Canadian Living
Essential Barbecue

EXCLUSIVE DISTRIBUTOR FOR CANADA & USA
Simon & Schuster Canada
166 King Street East, Suite 300
Toronto ON M5A 1J3
Tel: 647-427-8882
Toll Free: 800-387-0446   **simonandschuster.ca**
Fax: 647-430-9446   **canadianliving.com/books**

Cataloguing data available from
Bibliothèque et Archives nationales du Québec.

Art director: Colin Elliott
Editor: Martin Zibauer
Copy editor: Ruth Hanley
Indexer: Lisa Fielding

04-17

Legal deposit: 2017
Bibliothèque et Archives nationales du Québec
Library and Archives Canada

Printed in Canada

Government of Quebec – Tax credit for book publishing –
Administered by SODEC.
sodec.gouv.qc.ca

This publisher gratefully acknowledges the support of the
Société de développement des enterprises culturelles du Québec.

We gratefully acknowledge the support of the
Canada Council for the Arts for its publishing program.

We acknowledge the financial support of our publishing activities
by the Government of Canada through the Canada Book Fund.

Canadian Living
Essential Barbecue

BY THE CANADIAN LIVING TEST KITCHEN

JUNIPER
PUBLISHING
A Quebecor Media Corporation

Welcome to the
CANADIAN LIVING
TEST KITCHEN

You love to grill, and we want you to enjoy every hot and sizzling moment! Bringing you delicious, trustworthy recipes is the top priority for us in the Canadian Living Test Kitchen. We are chefs, recipe developers and food writers, all from different backgrounds but equally dedicated to the art and science of creating great recipes that you can make right at home.

WHAT DOES TESTED TILL PERFECT MEAN?

Every year, the food specialists in the Canadian Living Test Kitchen work together to produce approximately 500 Tested-Till-Perfect recipes. So what does Tested Till Perfect mean? It means we follow a rigorous process to ensure you'll get the same results in your kitchen as we do in ours.

HERE'S WHAT WE DO:

- In the Test Kitchen, we use the same everyday ingredients and equipment commonly found in kitchens across Canada.

- We start by researching ideas and brainstorming as a team.

- We write up the recipe and go straight into the kitchen to try it out.

- We taste, evaluate and tweak the recipe until we really love it.

- Once developed, each recipe gets handed off to other food editors for more testing and another tasting session.

- We meticulously test and retest each recipe as many times as it takes to make sure it turns out as perfectly in your kitchen as it does in ours.

- We carefully weigh and measure all ingredients, record the data and send the recipe out for nutritional analysis.

- The recipe is then edited and rechecked to ensure all the information is correct and it's ready for you to cook.

Grilling Essentials:
6 • Barbecue Success   **34** • Condiments

CONTENTS

Look for these helpful icons throughout the book

 QUICK & EASY
Ready in 30 minutes or less

 GRILLED APPETIZER
Starters and snacks

 COMPLETE MEAL
Fuss-free and satisfying

 VEGETARIAN DISHES
Fresh, meatless options

 CROWD-FRIENDLY
Great for entertaining

5 STEPS TO **BARBECUE SUCCESS**

1 Clean the grates

While your grill doesn't need to look shiny and new each time you use it, food residue on the grates can cause sticking. Because grates are easiest to clean when they're warm, tackle them after cooking or as the barbecue is heating. If you use a wire brush, check the bristles; they can break off and get into your food, where they can be dangerous. Safer alternatives include natural-fibre brushes, nylon scrubbers, and grill wipes.

② PREHEAT THE BARBECUE

Always preheat your grill for 10–15 minutes. A hot barbecue is essential to brown the food's surface—especially if you're using direct grilling.

CHOOSE THE RIGHT TECHNIQUE: DIRECT VS. INDIRECT

Grilling directly over the flame is usually the best choice for thin, small cuts, including steaks, kabobs and boneless skinless chicken pieces. Such cuts cook quickly, and need direct flame to brown the surface before the inside becomes overcooked.

For a large, thick cut—such as a roast or a Flintstones-size sirloin—use the indirect method: leave one burner unlit, preheat the adjacent burners, and place the meat over the unlit burner. (If you were to grill these over direct flame, the surface would dry out long before the inside cooks.)

To use indirect grilling with charcoal, create hot and cool zones by piling most of the coals on one side.

With indirect grilling, when the meat is almost done inside (use a thermometer to check), move it over the flame for a few minutes to brown and crisp the surface. Barbecue enthusiasts call this the "reverse-sear" or "two-stage" method. Indirect grilling also works well for foods that release fat and cause flare-ups, such as skin-on chicken pieces and pork ribs. Catch the fat in a foil drip pan set on the unlit burner.

4 Leave it be

When meat hits the grill, proteins can form a temporary bond with the metal grate. As the meat cooks, this bond will loosen, but if you try to move the meat too early, it can stick. Be patient; avoid shuffling food unless it's cooking unevenly or causing a flare-up.

USE A THERMOMETER

The most accurate way to check that meat is cooked properly is with an instant-read thermometer. Some models have a long, heat-resistant lead that connects the metal probe to a separate digital readout; the probe can stay in the food while it's cooking, and you can check the temperature without opening the barbecue lid. Some thermometers even transmit the temperature to an app on your phone—a very handy feature if you barbecue in winter.

When grilling steaks, burgers and sausages, check the internal temperature of several of them to ensure doneness; small, handheld instant-read thermometers work well for this task. To get an accurate temperature, always insert the probe into the thickest part of the food and avoid touching bone.

If you need to measure the temperature inside the barbecue chamber—as you would for smoking or baking in the barbecue—use an oven thermometer rather than relying on the gauge on the lid.

How do you like your steak?

RARE 135°F

Very soft; bright red centre

MEDIUM-RARE 145°F

Soft; pink inside with red centre

MEDIUM 160°F

Completely pink throughout

MEDIUM-WELL 165°F

Mostly brown inside;
hint of pink in the centre

WELL 165°F+

Firm; uniform brown throughout

Carryover cooking

After you take a steak off the grill, let
it rest for about five minutes; in that
time, its internal temperature will
continue to rise. A steak thinner than
¾ inch should come off the grill about
10°F shy of the desired doneness.
Remove a thicker steak about 5°F below
desired doneness.

The Ultimate Beef Burger

HANDS-ON TIME 20 MINUTES	TOTAL TIME 25 MINUTES	MAKES 6 SERVINGS

1 cup	fresh bread crumbs
⅔ cup	sodium-reduced beef broth
450 g	medium ground beef
450 g	ground sirloin
½ tsp	salt
¼ tsp	pepper
6	buns (hamburger, pretzel or pain au lait), split and toasted

In bowl, mix bread crumbs with broth; let stand for 5 minutes.

In large baking dish, add beef and sirloin; sprinkle with bread crumb mixture, salt and pepper. Mix gently just until combined and no streaks of bread crumb mixture are visible (do not overmix).

Shape into six ½-inch thick patties. *(Make-ahead: Layer between parchment paper in airtight container; refrigerate for up to 24 hours.)*

Place on greased grill over medium-high heat; close lid and grill, turning once, until instant-read thermometer inserted sideways into patties reads 160°F, 8 to 10 minutes. Serve in buns.

NUTRITIONAL INFORMATION, PER SERVING: about 416 cal, 34 g pro, 18 g total fat (7 g sat. fat), 28 g carb (1 g dietary fibre, 4 g sugar), 80 mg chol, 611 mg sodium, 388 mg potassium. % RDI: 8% calcium, 34% iron, 27% folate.

TIP FROM THE TEST KITCHEN

If you prefer thick, pub-style burgers, shape ground meat mixture into 1-inch patties. Place on greased grill over medium-high heat, close lid and grill for 7 minutes. Turn patties and reduce heat to medium; close lid and grill until instant-read thermometer inserted sideways into patties reads 160°F, about 7 minutes. Reducing the grill temperature partway through ensures the patties cook to a safe internal temperature without overcooking on the surface.

Turkish-Style Burgers

HANDS-ON TIME	TOTAL TIME	MAKES
15 MINUTES	25 MINUTES	4 SERVINGS

In bowl, stir together beef, tomato paste, egg, garlic, cumin, allspice, salt and hot pepper flakes. Add parsley and cilantro; mix gently just until combined. Shape into four ½-inch thick patties.

Place on greased grill over medium-high heat; brush with half of the molasses. Close lid and grill, turning once and brushing with remaining molasses, until instant-read thermometer inserted sideways into patties reads 160°F, 8 to 10 minutes. Sandwich with tomato and onion in buns.

NUTRITIONAL INFORMATION, PER SERVING: about 382 cal, 29 g pro, 14 g total fat (5 g sat. fat), 37 g carb (2 g dietary fibre, 11 g sugar), 101 mg chol, 580 mg sodium, 569 mg potassium. % RDI: 11% calcium, 31% iron, 9% vit A, 17% vit C, 46% folate.

VARIATION
Turkish-Style Lamb Burgers
Replace beef with ground lamb.

450 g	lean ground beef
2 tbsp	tomato paste
1	egg
1	clove garlic, grated
1 tsp	ground cumin
¼ tsp	ground allspice
¼ tsp	each salt and hot pepper flakes
2 tbsp	chopped fresh parsley
2 tbsp	chopped fresh cilantro
2 tbsp	pomegranate molasses
8	slices yellow or red tomato
⅓ cup	thinly sliced onion
4	soft white buns, split

Beef & Mushroom Cheeseburgers

HANDS-ON TIME	TOTAL TIME	MAKES
20 MINUTES	30 MINUTES	4 SERVINGS

8	cremini mushrooms
1	small onion, coarsely chopped
450 g	extra-lean ground beef
1 tsp	chopped fresh thyme
1 tsp	dry mustard
½ tsp	salt
¼ tsp	each black pepper and cayenne pepper
4	slices Cheddar cheese
2 cups	baby arugula
2	tomatoes, sliced
4	whole grain kaiser rolls, split and toasted

In food processor, finely chop mushrooms and onion; scrape into large bowl.

Add beef, thyme, mustard, salt, black pepper and cayenne pepper; mix gently just until combined. Shape into four ½-inch thick patties.

Place on greased grill over medium-high heat; close lid and grill, turning once, until instant-read thermometer inserted sideways into patties reads 160°F, 8 to 10 minutes.

Top each patty with Cheddar. Sandwich with arugula and tomatoes in rolls.

NUTRITIONAL INFORMATION, PER SERVING: about 451 cal, 36 g pro, 18 g total fat (8 g sat. fat), 39 g carb (7 g dietary fibre), 82 mg chol, 780 mg sodium, 914 mg potassium. % RDI: 25% calcium, 33% iron, 18% vit A, 22% vit C, 30% folate.

TIP FROM THE TEST KITCHEN

Using an instant-read thermometer is the best way to be sure burgers are cooked to a safe internal temperature. For an accurate reading, always insert the probe into the side of the patty, not the top.

Smoky Barbecue Patties

HANDS-ON TIME 15 MINUTES	TOTAL TIME 30 MINUTES	MAKES 4 SERVINGS

 In large bowl, beat egg with barbecue sauce; stir in bread crumbs, garlic, salt and pepper. Add beef; mix gently just until combined. Shape into four ¾-inch thick patties. (*Make-ahead: Layer between waxed paper in airtight container. Refrigerate for up to 24 hours; or freeze for up to 1 month and thaw in refrigerator.*)

Place on greased grill over medium heat; close lid and grill, turning once, until instant-read thermometer inserted sideways into patties reads 160°F, about 10 to 12 minutes.

NUTRITIONAL INFORMATION, PER SERVING: about 278 cal, 24 g pro, 14 g total fat (6 g sat. fat), 13 g carb (1 g dietary fibre), 108 mg chol, 388 mg sodium. % RDI: 5% calcium, 24% iron, 5% vit A, 3% vit C, 8% folate.

1	egg
⅓ cup	Smoky Barbecue Sauce (recipe follows)
⅓ cup	dried bread crumbs
2	cloves garlic, minced
¼ tsp	each salt and pepper
450 g	lean ground beef

Smoky Barbecue Sauce

In saucepan, whisk together 1 cup beef broth, 1 cup canned crushed tomatoes, ½ cup fancy molasses, 1 finely grated onion, 1 seeded and minced jalapeño pepper, 3 tbsp cider vinegar, 2 tbsp granulated sugar, 2 tbsp Dijon mustard, 4 tsp smoked paprika, 1 tsp ground cumin and ½ tsp each dried oregano, salt and pepper. Stir in ⅔ cup water; bring to boil. Reduce heat and simmer, stirring often, until reduced to 2 cups, about 20 minutes. (*Make-ahead: Let cool; refrigerate in airtight container for up to 2 weeks.*)

Sage-Rosemary Pork Burgers

HANDS-ON TIME	TOTAL TIME	MAKES
20 MINUTES	30 MINUTES	4 SERVINGS

2	green onions, chopped
2 tbsp	Dijon mustard
2	cloves garlic, minced
1 tsp	each dried sage and dried rosemary
½ tsp	each salt and pepper
450 g	lean ground pork
115 g	Gruyère cheese, shredded
half	red onion, cut in 4 slices
2 tsp	olive oil
4	hamburger buns, split and toasted

In large bowl, stir together green onions, mustard, garlic, sage, rosemary and half each of the salt and pepper. Add pork; mix gently just until combined. Shape into four ½-inch thick patties. Set aside.

Brush red onion all over with oil; sprinkle with remaining salt and pepper.

Place patties and onion slices on greased grill over medium-high heat; close lid and grill, turning once, until instant-read thermometer inserted sideways into patties reads 160°F and onion slices are softened, 8 to 10 minutes. Top burgers with Gruyère; close lid and cook, until Gruyère is melted, about 1 minute.

Sandwich burgers and onion rings in buns.

NUTRITIONAL INFORMATION, PER SERVING: about 506 cal, 36 g pro, 26 g total fat (11 g sat. fat), 32 g carb (2 g dietary fibre, 7 g sugar), 97 mg chol, 796 mg sodium, 509 mg potassium. % RDI: 37% calcium, 24% iron, 10% vit A, 10% vit C, 39% folate.

TIP FROM THE TEST KITCHEN
Since burgers shrink as they cook, shape the patties so they're slightly larger in diameter than the buns.

Pork Gyoza Burgers

HANDS-ON TIME	TOTAL TIME	MAKES
25 MINUTES	25 MINUTES	4 SERVINGS

In food processor, purée together egg, ginger, garlic, soy sauce, 2 tsp of the honey, pinch each of the salt and pepper and 1 tbsp water until smooth. Add mushrooms and green onions; pulse until finely chopped.

In bowl, add pork, mushroom mixture and bread crumbs; mix gently just until combined. Shape into four ½-inch thick patties. (*Make-ahead: Layer between waxed paper in airtight container. Refrigerate for up to 24 hours; or freeze for up to 3 weeks, adding 5 to 7 minutes to cook time.*) Place on greased grill over medium-high heat; close lid and grill, turning once, until instant-read thermometer inserted sideways into patties reads 160°F, 8 to 10 minutes.

While patties are grilling, in large bowl, whisk together sesame oil, vinegar and remaining honey, salt and pepper. Add coleslaw mix; toss to coat.

Spread mayonnaise over bottoms of buns. Sandwich patty and ½ cup of the coleslaw mixture in buns. Serve with remaining coleslaw on the side.

NUTRITIONAL INFORMATION, PER SERVING: about 635 cal, 32 g pro, 33 g total fat (12 g sat. fat), 54 g carb (3 g dietary fibre, 15 g sugar), 245 mg chol, 802 mg sodium, 446 mg potassium. % RDI: 7% calcium, 29% iron, 23% vit A, 28% vit C, 20% folate.

1	egg
1	piece (1 inch) fresh ginger, peeled and sliced
1	clove garlic
1 tbsp	sodium-reduced soy sauce
4 tsp	liquid honey
¼ tsp	each salt and pepper
1½ cups	stemmed shiitake mushrooms
4	green onions, chopped
450 g	lean ground pork
⅓ cup	panko or dried bread crumbs
2 tbsp	sesame oil
1 tbsp	white wine vinegar
3½ cups	coleslaw mix
4 tsp	light mayonnaise
4	brioche or pain au lait buns, split and toasted

TIP FROM THE TEST KITCHEN
Trim shiitake mushroom stems before cooking; the stems are too fibrous to eat, but you can use them to flavour soups and stocks.

Vegetarian Burgers

HANDS-ON TIME	TOTAL TIME	MAKES
20 MINUTES	35 MINUTES	4 SERVINGS

⅔ cup	quick-cooking (not instant) rolled oats
3 tbsp	vegetable oil
1	onion, diced
2	cloves garlic, chopped
1 tsp	dried thyme
¼ tsp	each salt and pepper
1	egg
4 tsp	Dijon mustard
1	pkg (340 g) precooked ground soy protein mixture
½ cup	mayonnaise
4	hamburger buns
4	leaves lettuce
8	slices tomato
4	slices Swiss cheese (optional)

In large dry skillet, toast oats over medium-high heat, stirring, until golden, about 3 minutes. Transfer to food processor; pulse until coarsely powdered.

In same skillet, heat 2 tbsp of the oil; cook onion, garlic, thyme, salt and pepper until light golden, about 4 minutes. Add to food processor.

Add egg and half of the mustard to food processor; pulse until combined. Transfer to bowl. Add ground soy protein; mix until combined. Shape into four ¾-inch patties.

Brush 1 side of each patty with some of the remaining oil; place, oiled side down, on greased grill over medium-high heat. Brush patties with remaining oil. Close lid and grill, turning once, until crisp and golden, 10 to 15 minutes.

Stir mayonnaise with remaining mustard; spread over buns. Sandwich lettuce, tomato, patties and Swiss (if using) in buns.

NUTRITIONAL INFORMATION, PER SERVING: about 626 cal, 26 g pro, 37 g total fat (5 g sat. fat), 48 g carb (9 g dietary fibre), 57 mg chol, 1,042 mg sodium, 686 mg potassium. % RDI: 16% calcium, 54% iron, 10% vit A, 15% vit C, 38% folate.

TIP FROM THE TEST KITCHEN
Look for ground soy protein near the tofu in the refrigerated section of your grocery store. To turn the burgers more easily, use two spatulas, placing one under and one over the patty. The same technique works well when grilling fish fillets.

Grilled Portobello Cheeseburgers

HANDS-ON TIME	TOTAL TIME	MAKES
10 MINUTES	25 MINUTES	4 SERVINGS

Remove stems and gills from mushrooms; wipe caps clean. Brush mushrooms and red onion with oil; sprinkle with salt and pepper.

Place mushrooms and red onion on greased grill over medium-high heat; close lid and grill, turning once, until tender and grill-marked, about 10 minutes. Transfer red onions to plate.

Add 1 slice provolone to each mushroom cap; close lid and grill, just until cheese is melted, about 2 minutes.

Meanwhile, spread red pepper spread over buns. Sandwich lettuce, tomato, mushrooms, red onion and basil leaves in buns.

NUTRITIONAL INFORMATION, PER SERVING: about 414 cal, 16 g pro, 25 g total fat (7 g sat. fat), 37 g carb (7 g dietary fibre), 23 mg chol, 704 mg sodium, 704 mg potassium. % RDI: 26% calcium, 15% iron, 21% vit A, 22% vit C, 22% folate.

4	large portobello mushrooms
4	thick slices red onion
3 tbsp	olive oil
¼ tsp	each salt and pepper
4	slices provolone cheese
⅓ cup	roasted red pepper spread or mayonnaise
4	whole wheat hamburger buns
4	leaves lettuce
8	slices tomato
8	leaves fresh basil

TIP FROM THE TEST KITCHEN
Instead of provolone, you can top the portobello with any cheese that melts well, such as Cheddar, Fontina, or Brie. But if you prefer a cheese that doesn't melt, such as feta, add it after your burger has cooked.

Herb & Cranberry Turkey Burger
WITH CARAWAY COLESLAW

HANDS-ON TIME	TOTAL TIME	MAKES
15 MINUTES	20 MINUTES	4 SERVINGS

BURGER

½ cup	quick-cooking (not instant) rolled oats
3	green onions, thinly sliced
¼ cup	dried cranberries, chopped
1	egg
1	clove garlic, grated or pressed
2 tbsp	chopped fresh parsley
1 tbsp	Dijon mustard
1 tbsp	cider vinegar
½ tsp	chopped fresh rosemary
¼ tsp	each salt and pepper
450 g	ground turkey
4	hamburger buns

SLAW

3 tbsp	cider vinegar
1 tbsp	olive oil
1 tbsp	Dijon mustard
1 tbsp	liquid honey
¼ tsp	caraway seeds
¼ tsp	pepper
pinch	salt
8 cups	coleslaw mix or broccoli slaw (about one 400 g pkg)
2 tbsp	chopped fresh parsley

BURGER In large bowl, stir together oats, green onions, cranberries, egg, garlic, parsley, mustard, vinegar, rosemary, salt, pepper and 2 tbsp water. Add turkey; mix gently just until combined. Shape into four ¾-inch thick patties.

Place on greased grill over medium-high heat; close lid and grill, turning once, until instant-read thermometer inserted sideways into patties reads 165°F, 10 to 12 minutes. Sandwich in buns.

SLAW Meanwhile, in large bowl, whisk together vinegar, oil, mustard, honey, caraway seeds, pepper and salt. Toss with coleslaw mix and parsley. Serve some on burgers and remainder on the side.

NUTRITIONAL INFORMATION, PER SERVING: about 480 cal, 30 g pro, 18 g total fat (4 g sat. fat), 52 g carb (6 g dietary fibre, 17 g sugar), 135 mg chol, 636 mg sodium, 458 mg potassium. % RDI: 15% calcium, 36% iron, 24% vit A, 57% vit C, 56% folate.

TIP FROM THE TEST KITCHEN
To grease a hot grill, dip a paper towel in a little vegetable oil. Using tongs, carefully wipe the towel over the grates. Keep a spray bottle filled with water on hand to douse flare-ups.

Butter Chicken Burgers

HANDS-ON TIME	TOTAL TIME	MAKES
15 MINUTES	20 MINUTES	4 SERVINGS

In bowl, stir together egg, garlic, bread crumbs, curry paste, lemon juice, ginger, garam masala, salt and pepper. Add chicken; mix gently just until combined. With wet hands, shape into four ¾-inch thick patties.

Place on greased grill over medium-high heat; close lid and grill, turning once, until instant-read thermometer inserted sideways into patties reads 165°F, 10 to 12 minutes.

NUTRITIONAL INFORMATION, PER SERVING: about 260 cal, 22 g pro, 14 g total fat (4 g sat. fat), 9 g carb (1 g dietary fibre), 121 mg chol, 388 mg sodium, 251 mg potassium. % RDI: 4% calcium, 15% iron, 6% vit A, 7% vit C, 10% folate.

1	egg
2	cloves garlic, minced
¼ cup	dried bread crumbs
2 tbsp	butter chicken curry paste
1 tbsp	lemon juice
2 tsp	grated fresh ginger
¾ tsp	garam masala
¼ tsp	each salt and pepper
450 g	ground chicken

TIP FROM THE TEST KITCHEN
Be sure to use thick butter chicken curry paste—not sauce—to keep the burgers moist but not sloppy.

Fresh Salmon Burgers
WITH TOMATO TARTAR SAUCE

HANDS-ON TIME	TOTAL TIME	MAKES
30 MINUTES	40 MINUTES	4 SERVINGS

TOMATO TARTAR SAUCE

½ cup	light mayonnaise
⅓ cup	finely chopped seeded tomato
1 tbsp	minced fresh parsley
1½ tsp	capers, finely chopped
½ tsp	lemon juice
dash	hot pepper sauce

BURGERS

450 g	salmon piece or fillets, skinned
1	small onion, grated
2 tbsp	dried bread crumbs
½ tsp	salt
¼ tsp	pepper
8	slices rye bread or 4 whole grain hamburger buns
4	leaves lettuce

TOMATO TARTAR SAUCE In small bowl, stir together mayonnaise, tomato, parsley, capers, lemon juice and hot pepper sauce. *(Make-ahead: Cover and refrigerate for up to 6 hours.)*

BURGERS Cut fish into chunks. In food processor, pulse together fish, ¼ cup of the tartar sauce, and the onion, bread crumbs, salt and pepper until finely chopped. Shape into four ¾-inch thick patties. *(Make-ahead: Layer between waxed paper in airtight container and refrigerate for up to 24 hours.)*

Place patties on greased grill over medium heat; close lid and grill, turning once, until golden and instant-read thermometer inserted sideways into patties reads 158°F, about 10 minutes.

Meanwhile, grill bread until slightly crisp, about 2 minutes. Sandwich lettuce, patties and remaining tartar sauce in bread.

NUTRITIONAL INFORMATION, PER SERVING: about 433 cal, 25 g pro, 23 g total fat (4 g sat. fat), 31 g carb (4 g dietary fibre), 69 mg chol, 926 mg sodium. % RDI: 7% calcium, 17% iron, 7% vit A, 17% vit C, 41% folate.

TIP FROM THE TEST KITCHEN

Before pulsing the salmon, run your fingers along the surface to check for bones; pull them out with tweezers. To remove skin, place fish on a cutting board, skin side down. At the narrow end, cut between the flesh and skin just enough so you can grip the skin with a paper towel. Angle the knife slightly down and pull the skin back and forth across the knife to cut between the skin and the flesh.

Salmon Burgers
WITH QUICK-PICKLED CUCUMBER

HANDS-ON TIME	TOTAL TIME	MAKES
35 MINUTES	1 HOUR	4 SERVINGS

QUICK-PICKLED CUCUMBER In bowl, combine cucumber, onion, vinegar and sugar; let stand for 30 minutes. Drain off liquid. *(Make-ahead: Cover and refrigerate for up to 4 hours.)*

SALMON BURGERS Meanwhile, peel and cut potatoes into chunks. In saucepan of boiling salted water, cover and cook potatoes until tender, about 15 minutes. Drain and return to pot; mash until smooth. Transfer to bowl.

Stir in dill, mustard, salt, lemon rind, pepper and egg. With fingers, break fish into pieces about size of rolled oats, removing any bones. Stir into potato mixture. Shape into four ¾-inch thick patties. Spread bread crumbs on plate; press patties into crumbs to coat both sides. *(Make-ahead: Cover and refrigerate for up to 24 hours.)*

Place patties on greased grill over medium heat; close lid and grill, turning once, until heated through and golden, about 10 minutes.

Meanwhile, cut buns in half; toast on grill for 2 minutes. Sandwich lettuce, patties and cucumber in bun.

NUTRITIONAL INFORMATION, PER SERVING: about 477 cal, 32 g pro, 9 g total fat (2 g sat. fat), 70 g carb (8 g dietary fibre), 121 mg chol, 1,406 mg sodium. % RDI: 33% calcium, 26% iron, 7% vit A, 25% vit C, 25% folate.

QUICK-PICKLED CUCUMBER

1 cup	thinly sliced cucumber
⅓ cup	thinly sliced sweet onion
2 tbsp	white wine vinegar
2 tsp	granulated sugar

SALMON BURGERS

2	large potatoes
2 tbsp	chopped fresh dill
1 tbsp	Dijon mustard
½ tsp	each salt and grated lemon rind
¼ tsp	pepper
1	egg, beaten
2	cans (each 213 g) salmon, drained
¼ cup	dried bread crumbs
4	whole grain hamburger buns
4	leaves lettuce

TIP FROM THE TEST KITCHEN
You can substitute 2 cups cooked salmon for the canned salmon.

Grilled Sausages
WITH PEPPERS & ONIONS

HANDS-ON TIME	TOTAL TIME	MAKES
20 MINUTES	20 MINUTES	6 SERVINGS

PEPPERS AND ONIONS
2	red onions
2	sweet red peppers
2	sweet yellow peppers
4 tsp	olive oil
¼ tsp	each salt and pepper

SAUSAGES
6	honey garlic sausages (about 600 g total)

PEPPERS AND ONIONS Slice red onions crosswise into ½-inch thick rounds. Slice red peppers and yellow peppers into ½-inch thick rings; remove seeds and white veins. Thread red onions onto metal or soaked wooden skewers; brush with half of the oil and sprinkle with half each of the salt and pepper. Toss together red peppers, yellow peppers and remaining oil, salt and pepper.

Place onion skewers and peppers on greased grill over medium-high heat; close lid and grill, turning occasionally, until tender and grill-marked, 10 to 15 minutes. *(Make-ahead: Refrigerate in airtight container for up to 3 days.)*

SAUSAGES Meanwhile, place sausages on greased grill over medium-high heat; close lid and grill, turning occasionally, until browned and juices run clear when sausage is pierced or instant-read thermometer inserted in sausages reads 160°F, about 12 minutes.

NUTRITIONAL INFORMATION, PER SERVING: about 386 cal, 16 g pro, 28 g total fat (9 g sat. fat), 18 g carb (2 g dietary fibre, 10 g sugar), 63 mg chol, 869 mg sodium. 307 mg potassium. % RDI: 4% calcium, 9% iron, 20% vit A, 350% vit C, 13% folate.

Sausage
WITH ISRAELI COUSCOUS & ESCAROLE

HANDS-ON TIME	TOTAL TIME	MAKES
30 MINUTES	35 MINUTES	4 SERVINGS

Place sausages and red onion on greased grill over medium-high heat; close lid and grill, turning occasionally, until red onions are slightly charred, 10 to 15 minutes.

Slice sausages in half lengthwise; grill, cut side down, until grill-marked, about 2 minutes. Coarsely chop red onion. Set sausages and onion aside.

Meanwhile, cook couscous according to package directions. In large bowl, toss together couscous, red onion, 1 tbsp of the oil and the vinegar.

In large skillet, heat remaining oil over medium-high heat; cook escarole, garlic, ¼ tsp of the salt and the hot pepper flakes, tossing frequently, until wilted, about 3 minutes. Add to couscous mixture and toss.

In same pan, heat tomatoes, shaking pan frequently, until tomatoes are softened, about 2 minutes. Add to couscous along with basil and remaining salt; toss to coat. Serve with sausages.

4	mild Italian sausages
half	red onion (with root end intact), cut in wedges
1 cup	Israeli (pearl) couscous
2 tbsp	extra-virgin olive oil
1 tbsp	balsamic vinegar
4 cups	coarsely chopped escarole
2	cloves garlic, thinly sliced
½ tsp	salt
¼ tsp	hot pepper flakes
2 cups	cherry tomatoes, halved
½ cup	fresh basil, thinly sliced

NUTRITIONAL INFORMATION, PER SERVING: about 542 cal, 22 g pro, 31 g total fat (8 g sat. fat), 45 g carb (5 g dietary fibre, 6 g sugar), 53 mg chol, 979 mg sodium, 809 mg potassium. % RDI: 8% calcium, 19% iron, 19% vit A, 23% vit C, 41% folate.

TIP FROM THE TEST KITCHEN
If you can't find escarole, you can substitute curly endive, dandelion or other greens.

TOPPINGS FOR GRILLED SAUSAGE

Kimchi Slaw

HANDS-ON TIME 5 MINUTES
TOTAL TIME 5 MINUTES
MAKES 6 SERVINGS

1 tbsp	seasoned rice vinegar
1 tsp	granulated sugar
1 tsp	sesame oil
⅔ cup	thinly sliced carrot
⅔ cup	thinly sliced seeded English cucumber
¼ cup	packed kimchi, drained and thinly sliced
3 tbsp	light mayonnaise
¼ tsp	sriracha sauce

In bowl, whisk together vinegar, sugar and oil until sugar is dissolved. Toss with carrot, cucumber and kimchi. *(Make-ahead: Cover and refrigerate overnight.)*

Combine mayonnaise with sriracha; drizzle over slaw just before serving.

NUTRITIONAL INFORMATION, PER SERVING: about 48 cal, trace pro, 3 g total fat (1 g sat. fat), 4 g carb (1 g dietary fibre, 3 g sugar), 3 mg chol, 206 mg sodium, 63 mg potassium. % RDI: 1% calcium, 1% iron, 24% vit A, 3% vit C, 2% folate.

Tomatillo Salsa

HANDS-ON TIME 10 MINUTES
TOTAL TIME 10 MINUTES
MAKES 6 SERVINGS

8	canned or fresh tomatillos
1	avocado, peeled, pitted and chopped
half	small red onion, diced
1	jalapeño pepper, minced
1	clove garlic, minced
2 tbsp	chopped fresh cilantro
2 tbsp	extra-virgin olive oil
2 tbsp	lime juice
pinch	each salt and pepper

Chop tomatillos; drain in colander.

In bowl, combine tomatillos, avocado, red onion, jalapeño pepper, garlic, cilantro, oil, lime juice, salt and pepper. *(Make-ahead: Refrigerate in airtight container for up to 24 hours. Drain before using.)*

NUTRITIONAL INFORMATION, PER SERVING: about 116 cal, 1 g pro, 10 g total fat (1 g sat. fat), 8 g carb (3 g dietary fibre, 3 g sugar), 0 mg chol, 6 mg sodium, 319 mg potassium. % RDI: 1% calcium, 4% iron, 1% vit A, 18% vit C, 16% folate.

Tomato Curry Topping

HANDS-ON TIME 10 MINUTES
TOTAL TIME 15 MINUTES
MAKES 6 SERVINGS

1 tbsp	vegetable oil
1	onion, chopped
2	cloves garlic, finely chopped
2 tsp	hot curry powder
1 can	(400 mL) diced tomatoes
2 tsp	each packed brown sugar and tomato paste
pinch	each salt and pepper

In saucepan, heat oil over medium heat; cook onion until beginning to soften, about 5 minutes.

Add garlic and curry powder; cook until fragrant, about 1 minute. Stir in tomatoes, brown sugar, tomato paste, salt and pepper; reduce heat to low and cook until reduced to 2 cups, about 5 minutes. *(Make-ahead: Cover and refrigerate up to 5 days.)*

NUTRITIONAL INFORMATION, PER SERVING: about 50 cal, 1 g pro, 3 g total fat (trace sat. fat), 7 g carb (1 g dietary fibre, 4 g sugar), 0 mg chol, 89 mg sodium, 188 mg potassium. % RDI: 3% calcium, 7% iron, 1% vit A, 18% vit C, 3% folate.

FROM TOP: **KIMCHI SLAW** (OPPOSITE),
TOMATILLO SALSA (OPPOSITE),
TOMATO CURRY TOPPING (OPPOSITE),
OKONOMIYAKI TOPPING (THIS PAGE)
AND **SPINACH DILL TZATZIKI** (P.32)

Okonomiyaki Topping

HANDS-ON TIME 45 MINUTES
TOTAL TIME 45 MINUTES
MAKES 6 SERVINGS

2 tbsp	butter
2	sweet onions, thinly sliced
2¼ tsp	granulated sugar
pinch	each salt and pepper
3 tbsp	ketchup
1 tbsp	Worcestershire sauce
1 tsp	sodium-reduced soy sauce
¼ tsp	Dijon mustard
¼ cup	each bonito flakes and sliced nori

In large skillet, melt butter over medium heat; cook onions, 2 tsp sugar, the salt and pepper, stirring occasionally, until onions are tender and golden, about 40 minutes.

Meanwhile, in small bowl, whisk together ketchup, Worcestershire sauce, soy sauce, remaining sugar and the mustard until sugar is dissolved. *(Make-ahead: Cover and refrigerate for up to 5 days.)* Just before serving, drizzle sauce over onions; sprinkle with bonito flakes and nori.

NUTRITIONAL INFORMATION, PER SERVING: about 87 cal, 1 g pro, 4 g total fat (2 g sat. fat), 13 g carb (1 g dietary fibre, 9 g sugar), 10 mg chol, 182 mg sodium, 200 mg potassium. % RDI: 3% calcium, 4% iron, 6% vit A, 13% vit C, 12% folate.

TOPPINGS FOR GRILLED SAUSAGE

Tahini Sauce

HANDS-ON TIME 5 MINUTES
TOTAL TIME 5 MINUTES
MAKES ¾ CUP

¼ **cup**	Balkan-style plain yogurt
¼ **cup**	tahini
2 **tbsp**	mayonnaise
1 **tbsp**	lemon juice
1	clove garlic, minced
¼ **tsp**	each paprika and salt

In small bowl, whisk together yogurt, tahini, mayonnaise, lemon juice, garlic, paprika, salt and 2 tbsp water until smooth. *(Make-ahead: Cover and refrigerate for up to 2 days.)*

NUTRITIONAL INFORMATION,
PER 1 TBSP: about 50 cal, 1 g pro, 5 g total fat (1 g sat. fat), 2 g carb (trace dietary fibre), 1 mg chol, 70 mg sodium. % RDI: 3% calcium, 4% iron, 1% vit A, 3% folate.

Spinach Dill Tzatziki

HANDS-ON TIME 5 MINUTES
TOTAL TIME 15 MINUTES
MAKES 6 SERVINGS

½ **cup**	shredded cucumber
¼ **tsp**	salt
½ **cup**	Greek-style plain yogurt
2 **tbsp**	frozen chopped spinach, thawed and squeezed dry
2	cloves garlic, minced
2 **tbsp**	chopped fresh dill
2 **tsp**	lemon juice
pinch	pepper
⅓ **cup**	crumbled feta cheese

Mix cucumber with pinch of the salt; let stand for 10 minutes. Squeeze out moisture.

In small bowl, mix together cucumber, yogurt, spinach, garlic, dill, lemon juice, pepper and remaining salt. *(Make-ahead: Cover and refrigerate for up to 2 days.)* Garnish with feta.

NUTRITIONAL INFORMATION,
PER SERVING: about 56 cal, 3 g pro, 4 g total fat (3 g sat. fat), 3 g carb (trace dietary fibre, 2 g sugar), 16 mg chol, 138 mg sodium, 108 mg potassium. % RDI: 9% calcium, 1% iron, 4% vit A, 3% vit C, 4% folate.

p.31

Caramelized Onions

HANDS-ON TIME 25 MINUTES
TOTAL TIME 25 MINUTES
MAKES ABOUT 1 CUP

1 **tbsp**	vegetable oil
1	Spanish onion, thinly sliced
1 **tbsp**	wine vinegar
1 **tsp**	granulated sugar
2	cloves garlic, thinly sliced
1 **tsp**	dried thyme
¼ **tsp**	each salt and pepper

In skillet, heat oil over medium-low heat; cook onion, vinegar, sugar, garlic, thyme, salt and pepper, stirring occasionally, for about 25 minutes or until caramelized. *(Make-ahead: Cover and refrigerate for up to 5 days.)*

NUTRITIONAL INFORMATION,
PER 1 TBSP: about 17 cal, trace pro, 1 g total fat (0 g sat. fat), 2 g carb (trace dietary fibre), 0 mg chol, 37 mg sodium. % RDI: 1% calcium, 1% iron, 1% folate.

Sausage Spiedini

HANDS-ON TIME	TOTAL TIME	MAKES
15 MINUTES	20 MINUTES	4 SERVINGS

Prick sausages with fork; place on microwaveable plate. Cover and microwave on high, turning once, until no longer pink, about 5 minutes. Cut into 1½-inch pieces.

Alternately thread sausage, bread and red onion onto skewers. Mix together oil, garlic, salt and pepper; brush over bread. Place skewers on grill over medium heat; close lid and grill, turning often, until browned and red onion is tender, about 10 minutes.

450 g	Italian sausages
1 piece	baguette (8 inches), cut in 1-inch cubes
half	red onion, cut in 1-inch pieces
2 tbsp	olive oil
1	clove garlic, pressed or minced
pinch	each salt and pepper

NUTRITIONAL INFORMATION, PER SERVING: about 354 cal, 19 g pro, 23 g total fat (7 g sat. fat), 17 g carb (1 g dietary fibre), 48 mg chol, 854 mg sodium. % RDI: 4% calcium, 14% iron, 5% vit C, 11% folate.

TIP FROM THE TEST KITCHEN

Fresh, or uncooked, sausages—including Italian sausages, bratwurst and English bangers—must be cooked until the juices run clear or an instant-read thermometer inserted into the sausages reads 160°F. Precooked sausages (look for "precooked" or "ready-to-eat" on the package), such as smokies or hot dogs, need only be heated through.

CONDIMENTS

Sweet Hot Mustard

HANDS-ON TIME 5 MINUTES
TOTAL TIME 5 MINUTES
MAKES 2 CUPS

1 cup	dry mustard
½ cup	packed brown sugar
½ cup	liquid honey
¼ cup	cider vinegar
3 tbsp	vegetable oil
½ tsp	kosher salt
½ tsp	lemon juice

In food processor, blend mustard with ¼ cup water until smooth paste forms. Add brown sugar, honey, vinegar, oil, salt and lemon juice; blend, scraping down side twice, until smooth, about 1 minute. Pack into hot (sterilized) 2-cup canning jar; seal tightly. Refrigerate; allow flavours to mellow for a few days before using. *(Make-ahead: Refrigerate for up to 1 month.)*

NUTRITIONAL INFORMATION, PER 1 TBSP: about 57 cal, 1 g pro, 2 g total fat (trace sat. fat), 8 g carb (trace dietary fibre, 8 g sugar), 0 mg chol, 26 mg sodium, 28 mg potassium. % RDI: 1% calcium, 2% iron, 2% vit C, 2% folate.

Chunky Tomato Pear Ketchup

HANDS-ON TIME 5 MINUTES
TOTAL TIME 1¼ HOURS
MAKES 1½ CUP

1 cup	chopped seeded peeled tomatoes
1	pear, peeled, cored and diced
1	green hot pepper
1	clove garlic, minced
¼ cup	golden raisins
3 tbsp	cider vinegar
2 tbsp	packed brown sugar
1 tbsp	tomato paste
1	cinnamon stick
¼ tsp	each salt and pepper

In saucepan, combine tomatoes, pear, hot pepper, garlic, raisins, vinegar, brown sugar, tomato paste, cinnamon stick, salt, pepper and ⅓ cup water; bring to boil. Reduce heat, cover and simmer, stirring occasionally, for 45 minutes.

Discard cinnamon stick and hot pepper; simmer, uncovered and breaking up some of the pear, until thickened, about 20 minutes. Let cool. *(Make-ahead: Refrigerate for up to 1 week.)*

NUTRITIONAL INFORMATION, PER 1 TBSP: about 15 cal, trace pro, 0 g total fat (0 g sat. fat), 4 g carb (trace dietary fibre, 3 g sugar), 0 mg chol, 26 mg sodium, 46 mg potassium. % RDI: 1% iron, 1% vit A, 2% vit C.

Homemade Mayonnaise

HANDS-ON TIME 5 MINUTES
TOTAL TIME 5 MINUTES
MAKES 1 CUP

1	egg, room temperature
2 tsp	Dijon mustard
¼ tsp	salt
¼ tsp	white or black pepper
1 cup	vegetable oil
2 tsp	lemon juice

In food processor, blend together egg, mustard, salt and pepper until smooth. With motor running, drizzle in 3 tbsp of the oil; gradually add remaining oil in thin steady stream until thickened. Add lemon juice; blend until smooth. *(Make-ahead: Refrigerate for up to 1 week.)*

NUTRITIONAL INFORMATION, PER 1 TBSP: about 112 cal, trace pro, 12 g total fat (1 g sat. fat), trace carb (trace dietary fibre, trace sugar), 11 mg chol, 43 mg sodium, 5 mg potassium. % RDI: 1% iron, 1% vit A, 1% folate.

VARIATION
Lemon Saffron Mayonnaise
Place pinch saffron threads in small heatproof bowl; pour in 1 tsp boiling water. Let stand for 10 minutes. Stir in ½ cup Homemade Mayonnaise, ¼ tsp grated lemon zest, 2 tsp lemon juice and pinch salt.

Salt & Pepper Steak
WITH GREEN SAUCE

HANDS-ON TIME	TOTAL TIME	MAKES
15 MINUTES	25 MINUTES	6 TO 8 SERVINGS

STEAK Sprinkle both sides of steak with salt and pepper; press to adhere. Place on greased grill over medium-high heat; close lid and grill, turning once, until medium-rare, 8 to 10 minutes.

Transfer to cutting board and tent with foil; let stand for 5 minutes before thinly slicing across the grain.

GREEN SAUCE Meanwhile, in food processor, pulse together cilantro, green onions, parsley, jalapeño pepper, garlic and 3 tbsp water until finely chopped; scrape into bowl. Stir in tomato, oil, vinegar, lemon juice and salt. Serve with steak.

NUTRITIONAL INFORMATION, PER EACH OF 8 SERVINGS: about 228 cal, 23 g pro, 14 g total fat (3 g sat. fat), 2 g carb (1 g dietary fibre), 53 mg chol, 413 mg sodium, 367 mg potassium. % RDI: 2% calcium, 19% iron, 6% vit A, 15% vit C, 8% folate.

VARIATION
Salt & Pepper Steak With Horseradish Cream
Omit Green Sauce. Drain ½ cup prepared horseradish in fine-mesh sieve, pressing to remove liquid; transfer to bowl. Stir in ½ cup mayonnaise, 3 tbsp sour cream and pinch pepper. Serve with steak.

STEAK

900 g	boneless beef grilling steak, about 1½ inches thick
1½ tsp	each coarse salt and pepper

GREEN SAUCE

1 cup	chopped fresh cilantro
½ cup	chopped green onions
⅓ cup	chopped fresh parsley
1	jalapeño pepper, seeded and finely chopped
1	clove garlic, minced
1	tomato, finely diced
⅓ cup	olive oil
3 tbsp	each red wine vinegar and lemon juice
¼ tsp	salt

Strip Loin Steak & Grilled Onions

HANDS-ON TIME	TOTAL TIME	MAKES
10 MINUTES	25 MINUTES	4 SERVINGS

⅓ **cup**	Dijon mustard
2 tbsp	chili powder
2 tsp	Worcestershire sauce
2	cloves garlic, minced
2	sweet onions (such as Vidalia or Spanish)
4	strip loin or other grilling steaks (each about 175 g)
½ **tsp**	each salt and pepper

Stir together mustard, chili powder, Worcestershire sauce and garlic; set aside.

Cut onions crosswise into scant ½-inch thick slices. Sprinkle both sides of steaks and onions with salt and pepper; brush mustard mixture onto one side of each. Place, mustard side down, on greased grill over medium-high heat; brush mustard mixture over tops.

Close lid and grill, turning once, until steaks reach desired doneness, about 8 minutes for medium-rare, and onions are browned and tender, about 1 minute longer per side. Transfer to warmed platter; tent with foil and let stand for 5 minutes before serving.

NUTRITIONAL INFORMATION, PER SERVING: about 405 cal, 35 g pro, 20 g total fat (7 g sat. fat), 22 g carb (4 g dietary fibre), 90 mg chol, 704 mg sodium. % RDI: 8% calcium, 30% iron, 13% vit A, 20% vit C, 17% folate.

TIP FROM THE TEST KITCHEN
Strip loin steaks are cut from the loin section. Though not as tender as steaks from the tenderloin (such as filets mignon), strip loins are much more flavourful.

Argentinian-Style Flank Steak & Carrots

HANDS-ON TIME	TOTAL TIME	MAKES
25 MINUTES	30 MINUTES	4 SERVINGS

FLANK STEAK

4	large carrots, peeled and sliced lengthwise ¼ inch thick
3 tsp	olive oil
¼ tsp	each salt and pepper
½ tsp	ground cumin
450 g	beef flank steak

CHIMICHURRI SAUCE

¾ cup	packed fresh parsley leaves
2	green onions, chopped
1	small clove garlic
2 tbsp	red wine vinegar
pinch	each salt and pepper
pinch	crushed hot pepper flakes
3 tbsp	extra-virgin olive oil

FLANK STEAK In large shallow dish, toss together carrots, 2 tsp of the oil and half each of the salt and pepper; set aside.

Combine cumin and remaining oil, salt and pepper; brush over both sides of steak. Place steak and carrots on greased grill over medium-high heat; close lid and grill, turning once, until steak is medium-rare, about 12 minutes, and carrots are tender, about 16 minutes. Transfer steak to cutting board; tent with foil. Let stand for 5 minutes before thinly slicing across the grain.

CHIMICHURRI SAUCE Meanwhile, in food processor, pulse together parsley, green onions, garlic, vinegar, salt, pepper and hot pepper flakes. With motor running, slowly drizzle in oil and 2 tbsp water. Serve with steak and carrots.

NUTRITIONAL INFORMATION, PER SERVING: about 323 cal, 25 g pro, 20 g total fat (5 g sat. fat), 9 g carb (3 g dietary fibre, 4 g sugar), 48 mg chol, 248 mg sodium, 534 mg potassium. % RDI: 5% calcium, 25% iron, 170% vit A, 33% vit C, 18% folate.

TIP FROM THE TEST KITCHEN

Flank steaks are large, relatively thin cuts that cook quickly on the grill. Use leftovers for tasty steak sandwiches: pile sliced steak, grilled vegetables and mayo on crusty rolls.

Steakhouse Rib Eyes
WITH BÉARNAISE SAUCE

HANDS-ON TIME	TOTAL TIME	MAKES
30 MINUTES	30 MINUTES	6 SERVINGS

BÉARNAISE SAUCE In small saucepan, bring shallot, vinegar, pepper and ¼ cup water to simmer over medium heat. Cook until reduced by half, about 3 minutes. Let cool.

In heatproof bowl, whisk egg yolks until pale; whisk in shallot mixture. Set bowl over saucepan of simmering water; cook, whisking constantly, until sauce is thick enough to coat back of spoon, about 5 minutes. Slowly drizzle in butter, whisking constantly. Whisk in tarragon. Remove saucepan from heat; set bowl of sauce over top to keep warm.

RIB EYES Brush both sides of steaks with oil and sprinkle with salt and pepper. Place on greased grill over medium-high heat; leave lid open and grill, turning at least twice, until instant-read thermometer inserted in centre reads 140°F, 10 to 12 minutes.

Transfer to rack and let rest, uncovered, for 5 minutes or until instant-read thermometer inserted in centre reads 145°F. Slice across the grain and serve with Béarnaise sauce.

NUTRITIONAL INFORMATION, PER SERVING: about 557 cal, 35 g pro, 45 g total fat (21 g sat. fat), trace carb (trace dietary fibre, trace sugar), 251 mg chol, 369 mg sodium, 408 mg potassium. % RDI: 3% calcium, 29% iron, 20% vit A, 12% folate.

BÉARNAISE SAUCE
1	shallot, finely chopped
2 tbsp	white wine vinegar
pinch	pepper
4	egg yolks
½ cup	butter, melted
1 tbsp	chopped fresh tarragon

RIB EYES
3	beef rib eye grilling steaks (each about 340 g and 1 inch thick)
2 tbsp	olive oil
½ tsp	each salt and pepper

VARIATION
Rib Eyes With Shallot-Herb Compound Butter
In skillet, melt 1 tbsp butter over medium heat; cook 1 cup chopped shallots and 4 cloves minced garlic until shallots are softened, about 6 minutes. Let cool. In bowl, stir together shallot mixture; ½ cup butter, softened; ¼ cup each chopped fresh basil and chopped fresh parsley; and 1 tbsp white wine vinegar. Scrape onto plastic wrap and shape into 1-inch thick log; wrap tightly. Refrigerate until firm, about 30 minutes. *(Make-ahead: Refrigerate for up to 3 days or freeze in freezer bag for up to 2 weeks.)* Cook steaks as directed; top with slices of compound butter.

Spicy Beef Lettuce Wraps

HANDS-ON TIME	TOTAL TIME	MAKES
25 MINUTES	25 MINUTES	4 SERVINGS

450 g	beef top sirloin grilling steak
¼ tsp	each salt and pepper
3 tbsp	lime juice
2 tbsp	canola oil
2 tsp	chili garlic sauce
1 tsp	grated fresh ginger
1 tsp	liquid honey
1 tsp	sodium-reduced soy sauce
1 tsp	sesame oil
1	sweet red pepper, thinly sliced
1 cup	julienned carrot
1 cup	julienned cucumber
2	green onions, thinly sliced
12	large leaves lettuce (such as leaf, iceberg, romaine or Boston)

Sprinkle steak with pinch each of the salt and pepper. Place on greased grill over medium-high heat; close lid and grill, turning once, until medium-rare, about 6 minutes. Let stand for 5 minutes before slicing.

Meanwhile, in large bowl, whisk together lime juice, canola oil, chili garlic sauce, ginger, honey, soy sauce, sesame oil and remaining salt and pepper. Stir in red pepper, carrot, cucumber and green onions. *(Make-ahead: Refrigerate for up to 24 hours.)* Just before serving, toss vegetables with steak; wrap in lettuce leaves.

NUTRITIONAL INFORMATION, PER SERVING: about 251 cal, 24 g pro, 13 g total fat (3 g sat. fat), 10 g carb (2 g dietary fibre, 5 g sugar), 53 mg chol, 279 mg sodium, 575 mg potassium. % RDI: 4% calcium, 21% iron, 84% vit A, 82% vit C, 20% folate.

TIP FROM THE TEST KITCHEN
The acid in the dressing will continue to cook the steak, so don't toss the salad until you're ready to eat. To keep the lettuce crisp, wrap it in damp paper towels and refrigerate it in an airtight container or plastic bag.

SPICE-RUBBED FLANK STEAK (OPPOSITE), **MUSHROOM SKEWERS** (P.123)
AND **GRILLED BAKED POTATOES WITH GREEN ONION SOUR CREAM** (P.147)

Spice-Rubbed Flank Steak

HANDS-ON TIME	TOTAL TIME	MAKES
20 MINUTES	4½ HOURS	12 TO 16 SERVINGS

 Whisk together garlic, ginger, oil, coriander, cumin, mustard and salt; set aside.

Using fork, prick steaks all over on both sides. Rub garlic mixture all over steaks. Place in large resealable plastic bag; seal bag and refrigerate for 4 hours. *(Make-ahead: Refrigerate for up to 24 hours.)*

Place steaks on greased grill over medium-high heat; leave lid open and grill, turning at least twice, until instant-read thermometer inserted in centres reads 140°F, 10 to 12 minutes. Transfer to rack and let stand, uncovered, for 5 minutes or until instant-read thermometer inserted in centres reads 145°F for medium-rare. Thinly slice across the grain.

NUTRITIONAL INFORMATION, PER EACH OF 16 SERVINGS: about 145 cal, 19 g pro, 7 g total fat (3 g sat. fat), 1 g carb (trace dietary fibre, trace sugar), 39 mg chol, 178 mg sodium, 194 mg potassium. % RDI: 1% calcium, 14% iron, 2% folate.

4	cloves garlic, finely grated or pressed
4 tsp	grated fresh ginger
4 tsp	olive oil
2 tsp	ground coriander
2 tsp	ground cumin
2 tsp	dry mustard
1 tsp	salt
2	beef flank marinating steaks (each about 650 g)

 TIP FROM THE TEST KITCHEN
Cooking for a crowd? A large steak is easier to grill and easier on your budget than several individual steaks. After the steaks rest, slice them and serve. Your guests can choose the well-done or the rare slices and eat as much or as little as they like.

Steak Sandwiches
WITH AVOCADO MAYO

HANDS-ON TIME	TOTAL TIME	MAKES
15 MINUTES	15 MINUTES	6 SERVINGS

AVOCADO MAYO

1	avocado, peeled, pitted and chopped
2 tbsp	light mayonnaise
pinch	salt

SANDWICHES

2 cups	lightly packed baby spinach
3½ cups	Grilled Peppers and Onions (see recipe, page 26)
1	Spice-Rubbed Flank Steak (see recipe, page 45), thinly sliced across the grain
6	long crusty sandwich rolls or pretzel buns, split and toasted

AVOCADO MAYO In small bowl, mash together avocado, mayonnaise and salt until smooth.

SANDWICHES Layer spinach, Grilled Peppers and Onions and Spice-Rubbed Flank Steak over bottom halves of rolls. Spread heaping 1 tbsp Avocado Mayo onto cut sides of top halves of rolls; sandwich with bottom halves.

NUTRITIONAL INFORMATION, PER SERVING: about 462 cal, 33 g pro, 18 g total fat (5 g sat. fat), 41 g carb (5 g dietary fibre, 6 g sugar), 53 mg chol, 626 mg sodium, 692 mg potassium. % RDI: 9% calcium, 36% iron, 19% vit A, 175% vit C, 49% folate.

VARIATION
Chive-Mustard Mayo
In small bowl, stir together ⅓ cup mayonnaise, 1 tbsp chopped fresh chives, 1 finely grated or pressed clove garlic, 1 tsp grainy mustard and 1 tsp lemon juice.

Tomato-Basil Mayo
In small bowl, stir together ⅓ cup mayonnaise; 2 tsp chopped drained oil-packed sun-dried tomatoes; 2 tsp lightly packed fresh basil leaves, finely chopped; and pinch salt.

Grilled Steak &
Asparagus Salad

HANDS-ON TIME	TOTAL TIME	MAKES
15 MINUTES	15 MINUTES	4 SERVINGS

p.158

SUN-DRIED TOMATO VINAIGRETTE Whisk together oil, vinegar, pesto and pepper.

SALAD Combine celery seeds, salt, pepper and garlic powder; rub all over steak. Brush red onion with some of the oil; toss asparagus with remaining oil to coat.

Place steak, red onion and asparagus on greased grill over medium-high heat; close lid and grill, turning once, until steak is medium-rare, red onion is softened and asparagus is tender-crisp, about 8 minutes. Transfer to cutting board. Let steak stand for 5 minutes before thinly slicing. Halve onion rings and asparagus.

In large bowl, add lettuce, red onion, asparagus and vinaigrette; toss to coat. Sprinkle with goat cheese. Top with steak.

NUTRITIONAL INFORMATION, PER SERVING: about 427 cal, 33 g pro, 26 g total fat (8 g sat. fat), 15 g carb (4 g dietary fibre, 7 g sugar), 64 mg chol, 339 mg sodium, 685 mg potassium. % RDI: 8% calcium, 32% iron, 57% vit A, 38% vit C, 92% folate.

SUN-DRIED TOMATO VINAIGRETTE

¼ cup	extra-virgin olive oil
3 tbsp	balsamic vinegar
2 tbsp	sun-dried tomato pesto
¼ tsp	pepper

SALAD

½ tsp	celery seeds
¼ tsp	each salt, pepper and garlic powder
450 g	beef strip loin grilling steak (1 inch thick)
1	red onion, cut in ½-inch thick rings
2 tsp	olive oil
1	bunch asparagus, trimmed
6 cups	torn hearts of romaine lettuce (about 200 g)
70 g	pepper-coated goat cheese, crumbled

TIP FROM THE TEST KITCHEN
Letting steak rest before slicing gives the juices a chance to redistribute and settle within the steak. When you cut the steak, more juices will stay in the meat and not on the cutting board.

Steak & Potato Salad

HANDS-ON TIME	TOTAL TIME	MAKES
25 MINUTES	30 MINUTES	4 SERVINGS

VINAIGRETTE

2 tbsp	extra-virgin olive oil
1 tbsp	white wine vinegar
1 tsp	Dijon mustard
pinch	each salt and pepper

SALAD

2 tbsp	olive oil
1 tsp	each paprika and dried oregano
¼ tsp	each salt and pepper
450 g	mini red-skinned potatoes (about 16)
450 g	beef flank steak
8 cups	lightly packed mixed baby greens
1 cup	thinly sliced fennel bulb
1 cup	halved grape tomatoes
¼ cup	crumbled blue cheese

VINAIGRETTE Whisk together oil, vinegar, mustard, salt and pepper; set aside.

SALAD In small bowl, stir together oil, paprika, oregano, salt and pepper; set aside.

Scrub and halve potatoes. Place in microwaveable dish; sprinkle with 2 tbsp water. Cover and microwave on high until tender, 5 to 8 minutes. Toss with half of the paprika mixture; thread onto metal skewers.

Rub remaining paprika mixture all over steak. Place steak and potatoes on greased grill over medium-high heat; close lid and grill, turning once, until steak is medium-rare and potatoes are tender, 10 to 12 minutes. Transfer steak to cutting board; let stand for 5 minutes before thinly slicing across the grain. Remove potatoes from skewers.

In large bowl, add greens, fennel, tomatoes, potatoes, steak and vinaigrette; toss to coat. Sprinkle with blue cheese.

NUTRITIONAL INFORMATION, PER SERVING: about 428 cal, 30 g pro, 23 g total fat (6 g sat. fat), 25 g carb (5 g dietary fibre, 3 g sugar), 55 mg chol, 366 mg sodium, 1,231 mg potassium. % RDI: 14% calcium, 31% iron, 31% vit A, 67% vit C, 58% folate.

TIP FROM THE TEST KITCHEN

In the Test Kitchen, we prefer medium-rare steaks. If you've cooked your steak to medium or well-done, slice it very thinly to keep the fibres short and easy to chew.

Grilled Pork Chops
WITH OLIVE SALSA & HERBED COUSCOUS

HANDS-ON TIME	TOTAL TIME	MAKES
15 MINUTES	20 MINUTES	4 SERVINGS

OLIVE SALSA In small bowl, stir together tomatoes, red onion, olives, oregano, oil and vinegar.

PORK CHOPS Sprinkle pork with salt and pepper. Place on greased grill over medium-high heat; close lid and grill, turning once, until juices run clear when pork is pierced and just a hint of pink remains inside, 10 to 12 minutes.

HERBED ISRAELI COUSCOUS In saucepan, bring 1¾ cups water to boil; add Israeli couscous. Cover and simmer until no liquid remains, about 8 minutes. Stir in butter, parsley, mint, salt and pepper. Serve with pork chops and salsa.

NUTRITIONAL INFORMATION, PER SERVING: about 480 cal, 34 g pro, 14 g total fat (6 g sat. fat), 54 g carb (3 g dietary fibre, 2 g sugar), 67 mg chol, 332 mg sodium, 555 mg potassium. % RDI: 5% calcium, 18% iron, 11% vit A, 15% vit C, 22% folate.

OLIVE SALSA

½ cup	chopped grape tomatoes
⅓ cup	finely diced red onion
⅓ cup	sliced pitted black olives
2 tbsp	chopped fresh oregano
1 tbsp	extra-virgin olive oil
1 tbsp	red wine vinegar

PORK CHOPS

4	boneless centre-cut fast-fry pork chops (about 450 g total)
pinch	each salt and pepper

HERBED ISRAELI COUSCOUS

1½ cups	Israeli (pearl) couscous
2 tbsp	butter or extra-virgin olive oil
¼ cup	chopped fresh parsley
1 tbsp	chopped fresh mint
¼ tsp	each salt and pepper

TIP FROM THE TEST KITCHEN
Israeli, or pearl, couscous is much larger than the more common North African couscous and has a slightly chewy texture. It's usually cooked like pasta or rice.

Bacon-Stuffed Pork Chops

HANDS-ON TIME	TOTAL TIME	MAKES
40 MINUTES	40 MINUTES	4 SERVINGS

6	slices sodium-reduced bacon
1	small onion, finely chopped
2	cloves garlic, minced
¼ cup	dry white wine
2 cups	cubed whole wheat bread
¼ cup	each chopped fresh basil and fresh oregano
¼ cup	grated Parmesan cheese
4	boneless pork chops (about 450 g total)
1 tsp	olive oil
¼ tsp	pepper
pinch	salt

In large nonstick skillet, cook bacon over medium-high heat until slightly crisp, 5 to 8 minutes. Transfer to paper towel–lined plate to drain; coarsely chop.

Drain all but 1 tsp fat from pan; cook onion, stirring frequently, until softened, about 5 minutes. Add garlic; cook until fragrant, about 1 minute. Add wine; cook, stirring and scraping up browned bits, until reduced by half, about 30 seconds. Turn off heat.

Add bread and ⅓ cup water to pan; cook, stirring, until liquid is absorbed and moist stuffing holds together, adding up to 2 tbsp more water, if necessary. Remove from heat. Stir in basil, oregano, Parmesan and bacon. Let cool slightly.

With knife held horizontally and starting at rounded edge, cut wide pocket in each chop. Fill each pocket with one-quarter of the stuffing. Brush with oil; sprinkle with pepper and salt.

Place chops on greased grill over medium-high heat; close lid and grill, turning once, until juices run clear when pork is pierced and just a hint of pink remains inside, 10 to 12 minutes.

NUTRITIONAL INFORMATION, PER SERVING: about 288 cal, 34 g pro, 11 g total fat (4 g sat. fat), 11 g carb (2 g dietary fibre, 4 g sugar), 71 mg chol, 419 mg sodium, 432 mg potassium. % RDI: 10% calcium, 13% iron, 3% vit A, 3% vit C, 7% folate.

TIP FROM THE TEST KITCHEN
Be careful not to overcook pork chops, which can become dry when grilled. Stuffing them adds moisture—or, serve with a sauce or salsa.

Sticky Lamb Chops
WITH PARMESAN CAULIFLOWER

HANDS-ON TIME	TOTAL TIME	MAKES
15 MINUTES	15 MINUTES	4 SERVINGS

LAMB Whisk together honey, garlic, lime juice and mustard; set aside.

Sprinkle lamb with salt and pepper. Place on greased grill over medium-high heat; close lid and grill, turning once, until desired doneness, about 5 minutes for medium-rare. Brush all over with honey mixture; cook until glazed and sticky, 1 to 2 minutes.

PARMESAN CAULIFLOWER While lamb is cooking, in steamer basket set over saucepan of boiling water, steam cauliflower, covered, until tender-crisp, about 5 minutes.

In large bowl, stir together Parmesan, parsley, olives, oil, lime juice, salt and pepper. Stir in cauliflower. Serve with lamb.

NUTRITIONAL INFORMATION, PER SERVING: about 378 cal, 24 g pro, 25 g total fat (9 g sat. fat), 16 g carb (4 g dietary fibre, 11 g sugar), 54 mg chol, 376 mg sodium, 456 mg potassium. % RDI: 11% calcium, 15% iron, 4% vit A, 108% vit C, 35% folate.

LAMB

2 tbsp	liquid honey
2	cloves garlic, finely grated or pressed
2 tsp	lime juice
1 tsp	Dijon mustard
8	frenched lamb chops (about 565 g total)
¼ tsp	each salt and pepper

PARMESAN CAULIFLOWER

1	small head cauliflower, cut in bite-size florets
¼ cup	grated Parmesan cheese
¼ cup	chopped fresh parsley
2 tbsp	finely chopped pitted Niçoise olives
2 tbsp	extra-virgin olive oil
1 tbsp	lime juice
pinch	each salt and pepper

TIP FROM THE TEST KITCHEN
Frenched lamb chops (ask your butcher for them) have the meat scraped off the long bones—making an elegant handle when you just can't resist picking up the chops.

Rosemary-Dijon Lamb Chops
WITH SMASHED POTATOES

HANDS-ON TIME	TOTAL TIME	MAKES
25 MINUTES	30 MINUTES	4 SERVINGS

900 g	potatoes, peeled and quartered
6	cloves garlic
3 tbsp	extra-virgin olive oil
1 tsp	pepper
¾ tsp	salt
¼ cup	chopped fresh chives
2 tbsp	finely chopped fresh rosemary
1 tbsp	Dijon mustard
8	lamb chops (about 565 g total)

In saucepan of boiling salted water, cook potatoes and 4 of the garlic cloves until potatoes are tender, about 15 minutes. Reserving ½ cup of the cooking liquid, drain; transfer potatoes and garlic to large bowl. Add reserved cooking liquid, oil and half each of the pepper and salt; smash with potato masher until smooth with a few chunks remaining. Stir in chives. Keep warm.

Mince remaining garlic. Combine garlic, rosemary, mustard and remaining pepper and salt. Rub all over chops. Place on greased grill over medium-high heat; close lid and grill, turning once, until desired doneness, about 5 minutes for medium-rare. Serve with potatoes.

NUTRITIONAL INFORMATION, PER SERVING: about 366 cal, 18 g pro, 16 g total fat (4 g sat. fat), 39 g carb (3 g dietary fibre, 2 g sugar), 32 mg chol, 1,014 mg sodium, 805 mg potassium. % RDI: 4% calcium, 14% iron, 2% vit A, 27% vit C, 13% folate.

TIP FROM THE TEST KITCHEN
All grills have hot spots, which are prone to flare-ups. If lamb chops—or other foods—cause a flare-up, just move the food away from the flame to a cooler part of the grill.

RUBS

All-Purpose Rub

HANDS-ON TIME 5 MINUTES
TOTAL TIME 5 MINUTES
MAKES ½ CUP

3 tbsp	paprika
1 tbsp	packed brown sugar
2 tsp	each garlic powder and ground cumin
1 tsp	each salt, black pepper, dried oregano and onion powder
½ tsp	dry mustard
¼ tsp	cayenne pepper

In small bowl, stir together paprika, brown sugar, garlic powder, cumin, salt, black pepper, oregano, onion powder, dry mustard and cayenne pepper. *(Make-ahead: Store in airtight container for up to 3 months.)*

NUTRITIONAL INFORMATION, PER 2 TBSP: about 42 cal, 1 g pro, 1 g total fat (trace sat. fat), 9 g carb (3 g dietary fibre, 4 g sugar), 0 mg chol, 579 mg sodium, 190 mg potassium. % RDI: 3% calcium, 17% iron, 25% vit A, 8% vit C, 4% folate.

Jerk Seasoning

HANDS-ON TIME 5 MINUTES
TOTAL TIME 5 MINUTES
MAKES ⅓ CUP

2 tbsp	dried thyme
2 tsp	each salt, black pepper and garlic powder
1 tsp	each cinnamon, ground coriander and ground ginger
¾ tsp	cayenne pepper
½ tsp	each ground allspice and nutmeg

In bowl, mix together thyme, salt, black pepper, garlic powder, cinnamon, coriander, ginger, cayenne pepper, allspice and nutmeg. *(Make-ahead: Store in airtight container for up to 3 months.)*

NUTRITIONAL INFORMATION, PER 2 TBSP: about 31 cal, 1 g pro, 1 g total fat (trace sat. fat), 7 g carb (3 g dietary fibre, 1 g sugar), 0 mg chol, 1,724 mg sodium, 106 mg potassium. % RDI: 8% calcium, 36% iron, 3% vit A, 5% vit C, 5% folate.

Pepper-Coriander Rub

HANDS-ON TIME 7 MINUTES
TOTAL TIME 7 MINUTES
MAKES ⅓ CUP

2 tbsp	each coriander seeds and black peppercorns
2 tsp	each coarse salt and dehydrated minced garlic

In dry skillet, toast coriander seeds and peppercorns over medium heat, shaking pan frequently, until fragrant, about 4 minutes. Let cool.

In spice mill or coffee grinder, coarsely grind together coriander seeds, peppercorns and salt. Transfer to small bowl; stir in garlic. *(Make-ahead: Store in airtight container for up to 3 months.)*

NUTRITIONAL INFORMATION, PER 2 TBSP: about 31 cal, 1 g pro, 1 g total fat (trace sat. fat), 7 g carb (3 g dietary fibre, trace sugar), 0 mg chol, 1,164 mg sodium, 112 mg potassium. % RDI: 5% calcium, 16% iron, 3% vit C.

HOW TO

For 4 servings—450 g boneless (or 675 g bone-in) meat or poultry, or 450 g fish—use about 2 tbsp rub. Let stand at room temperature for 15 minutes before grilling. *(Make-ahead: Cover and refrigerate for up to 24 hours before grilling.)*

The Ultimate Barbecue-Smoked Ribs

HANDS-ON TIME	TOTAL TIME	MAKES
45 MINUTES	4 HOURS	6 TO 8 SERVINGS

RIBS

2	racks pork back ribs (about 1.8 kg total)
4 tsp	chili powder
2 tsp	packed brown sugar
2 tsp	ground cumin
1 tsp	garlic powder
½ tsp	pepper

MOLASSES BARBECUE SAUCE

1 tsp	vegetable oil
1	small sweet onion, finely diced
2	cloves garlic, minced
1 tsp	smoked paprika
¾ cup	ketchup
2 tbsp	cooking molasses
¼ tsp	pepper

RIBS Remove membrane (if attached) from underside of ribs. Combine chili powder, sugar, cumin, garlic powder and pepper; rub all over ribs. Cover and refrigerate for 2 hours. *(Make-ahead: Refrigerate for up to 24 hours.)*

Soak 3 cups wood chips in water for 1 hour; drain. Set foil drip pan under 1 rack of 2-burner barbecue or under centre rack of 3-burner barbecue. Heat remaining burner(s) to medium heat. (For charcoal barbecue, set a drip pan in the centre, with hot coals on either side.)

Seal soaked wood chips in heavy-duty foil to make packet; poke several holes in top. Remove one rack and place packet directly over lit burner; close lid. (For charcoal barbecue, place soaked chips directly on coals.)

Place ribs, meaty side down, on greased grill over drip pan; close lid and grill, turning once, until meat is tender and pulls away from ends of bones, about 1½ hours.

MOLASSES BARBECUE SAUCE Meanwhile, in saucepan, heat oil over medium heat; cook onion, garlic and paprika, stirring, until softened, about 5 minutes. Stir in ketchup, ¼ cup water, the molasses and pepper; reduce heat and simmer until slightly thickened, about 3 minutes. *(Make-ahead: Refrigerate in airtight container for up to 3 days.)*

Brush about half of the sauce over both sides of ribs. Close lid and grill over medium-high direct heat, turning once, until glazed, about 10 minutes. Cut into 2-rib portions. Serve with remaining sauce.

NUTRITIONAL INFORMATION, PER EACH OF 8 SERVINGS: about 399 cal, 27 g pro, 26 g total fat (10 g sat. fat), 15 g carb (1 g dietary fibre, 11 g sugar), 103 mg chol, 390 mg sodium, 557 mg potassium. % RDI: 6% calcium, 16% iron, 7% vit A, 10% vit C, 5% folate.

Five-Spice Pork Ribs

HANDS-ON TIME	TOTAL TIME	MAKES
25 MINUTES	3 HOURS	4 TO 6 SERVINGS

FIVE-SPICE RUB Combine five-spice powder, coriander, brown sugar, garlic powder and pepper.

RIBS Remove membrane (if attached) from underside of ribs. Rub spice mixture all over ribs, massaging into meat. Cover and refrigerate for 1 hour. *(Make-ahead: Refrigerate for up to 24 hours.)*

Set foil drip pan under 1 rack of 2-burner barbecue or under centre rack of 3-burner barbecue. Heat remaining burner(s) to medium heat.

Place ribs, meaty side down, on greased grill over drip pan; close lid and grill, turning once, until meat is tender and pulls away from ends of bones, about 1½ hours.

In saucepan, heat oil over medium heat; cook green onions, garlic and ginger until fragrant, about 1 minute. Add orange juice, hoisin sauce, vinegar and salt; bring to boil. Reduce heat and simmer until glaze is thickened slightly, about 3 minutes.

Transfer ribs to direct heat; brush with some of the glaze. Leave lid open and grill, turning ribs and brushing with glaze, until slightly sticky, about 10 minutes. Cut into 1- or 2-rib portions.

NUTRITIONAL INFORMATION, PER EACH OF 6 SERVINGS: about 443 cal, 31 g pro, 30 g total fat (11 g sat. fat), 11 g carb (1 g dietary fibre, 6 g sugar), 120 mg chol, 317 mg sodium, 458 mg potassium. % RDI: 7% calcium, 15% iron, 1% vit A, 12% vit C, 6% folate.

FIVE-SPICE RUB

1 tbsp	five-spice powder
2 tsp	ground coriander
2 tsp	packed brown sugar
1 tsp	garlic powder
1 tsp	pepper

RIBS

2	racks pork back ribs (about 1.5 kg total)
1 tsp	vegetable oil
3	green onions, thinly sliced
3	cloves garlic, minced
2 tsp	grated fresh ginger
⅓ cup	orange juice
¼ cup	hoisin sauce
1 tbsp	rice vinegar
pinch	salt

TIP FROM THE TEST KITCHEN

Five-spice powder is a classic Chinese mix—usually ground cinnamon, star anise, fennel, Szechuan pepper and cloves, balanced so no single flavour dominates. Try this five-spice rub on grilled chicken or turkey.

Rosemary-Garlic Baby Back Ribs

HANDS-ON TIME	TOTAL TIME	MAKES
15 MINUTES	2¼ HOURS	6 TO 8 SERVINGS

2	racks pork back ribs (about 1.8 kg total)
4	cloves garlic, minced
¼ cup	chopped fresh rosemary
2 tbsp	olive oil
2 tsp	salt
1 tsp	hot pepper flakes
1 tsp	pepper
2	lemons, quartered

Remove membrane (if attached) from underside of ribs; cut racks into 4 sections.

In large dish, combine garlic, rosemary, oil, salt, hot pepper flakes and pepper. Add ribs and rub all over with spice mixture. Cover and refrigerate for 1 hour. *(Make-ahead: Refrigerate for up to 24 hours.)*

Set foil drip pan under 1 rack of 2-burner barbecue or under centre rack of 3-burner barbecue. Heat remaining burner(s) to medium heat.

Place ribs, meaty side down, on greased grill over drip pan. Close lid and grill, turning once, until meat is tender and pulls away from ends of bones, about 1 hour. Squeeze lemon over ribs before serving.

8+

NUTRITIONAL INFORMATION, PER EACH OF 8 SERVINGS: about 370 cal, 26 g pro, 28 g total fat (10 g sat. fat), 2 g carb (trace dietary fibre), 103 mg chol, 696 mg sodium, 339 mg potassium. % RDI: 4% calcium, 9% iron, 2% vit A, 10% vit C, 2% folate.

TIP FROM THE TEST KITCHEN
If you are using a charcoal barbecue, place drip pan in the centre of grill and arrange hot coals on either side of drip pan. Set meat on greased grill over drip pan and grill as directed.

Caribbean-Style Pork Ribs
WITH QUICK PINEAPPLE RELISH

HANDS-ON TIME	TOTAL TIME	MAKES
30 MINUTES	4½ HOURS	6 TO 8 SERVINGS

RIBS Remove membrane (if attached) from underside of ribs. Combine thyme, garlic powder, coriander, salt, cayenne pepper, black pepper, ginger, allspice and nutmeg. Rub all over ribs. Cover and refrigerate for 2 hours. *(Make-ahead: Refrigerate for up to 24 hours.)*

Set foil drip pan under 1 rack of 2-burner barbecue or under centre rack of 3-burner barbecue. Heat remaining burner(s) to medium heat.

Place ribs, meaty side down, on greased grill over drip pan; close lid and grill, turning once, until meat is tender and pulls away from ends of bones, about 1¾ hours.

PINEAPPLE RELISH Meanwhile, in saucepan, heat oil over medium-high heat; cook onion, garlic and ginger until softened, about 3 minutes. Add crushed pineapple and its juice, jalapeño pepper, vinegar, salt and pepper; cook, stirring occasionally, for 3 minutes.

Blend cornstarch with 2 tbsp water; stir into pineapple mixture and boil, stirring constantly, until thickened, about 1 minute. Stir in green onion. Let cool. *(Make-ahead: Cover and refrigerate for up to 2 days.)* Serve with ribs.

NUTRITIONAL INFORMATION, PER EACH OF 8 SERVINGS: about 419 cal, 25 g pro, 30 g total fat (11 g sat. fat), 11 g carb (1 g dietary fibre, 8 g sugar), 108 mg chol, 402 mg sodium, 425 mg potassium. % RDI: 6% calcium, 16% iron, 2% vit A, 8% vit C, 5% folate.

RIBS
2	racks pork back ribs (about 1.8 kg total)
1 tbsp	dried thyme
1 tsp	each garlic powder and ground coriander
¾ tsp	salt
½ tsp	each cayenne pepper, black pepper, ground ginger and ground allspice
pinch	nutmeg

PINEAPPLE RELISH
2 tsp	vegetable oil
1	small onion, diced
2	cloves garlic, chopped
1 tsp	minced fresh ginger
1 can	(400 mL) crushed pineapple (undrained)
1	jalapeño pepper, seeded and finely chopped
1 tbsp	vinegar
¼ tsp	each salt and pepper
1 tsp	cornstarch
1	green onion, thinly sliced

TIP FROM THE TEST KITCHEN

The membrane on the concave, bony underside of the ribs is also called the "silverskin." To remove it, lift a corner, then grab with a paper towel and peel it off.

Stout-Glazed Beef Ribs

HANDS-ON TIME	TOTAL TIME	MAKES
40 MINUTES	2 HOURS	4 SERVINGS

2 kg	beef back ribs, cut in 1-rib portions
½ tsp	each salt and pepper
2	bottles (341 mL each) stout
1	onion, sliced
3	cloves garlic, sliced
½ cup	packed brown sugar
¼ cup	tomato paste
3 tbsp	drained prepared horseradish
2 tbsp	Dijon mustard
1 tbsp	Worcestershire sauce

Sprinkle ribs all over with salt and pepper; place in roasting pan, meaty side down. Add stout, onion and garlic; cover and braise in 325°F oven until fork tender, about 1¼ hours.

Transfer ribs to plate. Skim fat from braising liquid; strain liquid through fine-mesh sieve; discard solids. Pour 1½ cups braising liquid into saucepan; whisk in brown sugar, tomato paste, horseradish, mustard and Worcestershire sauce. Bring to boil over medium-high heat, whisking frequently; cook until thickened and reduced to 1 cup, about 15 minutes.

Place ribs on greased grill over medium-high heat; close lid and grill, basting with sauce every few minutes, until caramelized, 12 to 15 minutes.

NUTRITIONAL INFORMATION, PER SERVING: about 484 cal, 31 g pro, 22 g total fat (10 g sat. fat), 38 g carb (1 g dietary fibre, 30 g sugar), 75 mg chol, 473 mg sodium, 728 mg potassium. % RDI: 7% calcium, 27% iron, 2% vit A, 12% vit C, 11% folate.

TIP FROM THE TEST KITCHEN
You can make this recipe with pork ribs instead of beef—just cut them into 2-rib portions and add 1 hour to the braising time.

Grilled Korean Beef Ribs

HANDS-ON TIME	TOTAL TIME	MAKES
30 MINUTES	8½ HOURS	6 TO 8 SERVINGS

Chop 3 green onions. In blender, purée together chopped green onions and the pear, soy sauce, vinegar, sugar, ginger, garlic, pepper, oil and salt.

Place ribs in large shallow dish and pour marinade over top. Cover and refrigerate for at least 8 hours or up to 24 hours, turning ribs occasionally.

Place ribs on greased grill over medium-high heat; close lid and grill, turning once, until still slightly pink in centre, about 6 minutes.

Thinly slice remaining green onion. Slice ribs into 1- or 2-rib sections and sprinkle with green onion.

NUTRITIONAL INFORMATION, PER EACH OF 8 SERVINGS: about 362 cal, 19 g pro, 29 g total fat (12 g sat. fat), 5 g carb (1 g dietary fibre, 3 g sugar), 63 mg chol, 298 mg sodium, 211 mg potassium. % RDI: 2% calcium, 13% iron, 1% vit A, 2% vit C, 4% folate.

4	green onions
1	small Asian pear, peeled and cubed
¼ cup	sodium-reduced soy sauce
2 tbsp	unseasoned rice wine vinegar
2 tbsp	granulated sugar
1	piece ginger (1-inch), peeled and sliced
4	cloves garlic
1 tsp	pepper
¾ tsp	sesame oil
¼ tsp	salt
1.3 kg	Korean-style beef short ribs

TIP FROM THE TEST KITCHEN
Thinly sliced Korean-style beef ribs are also called "Miami-style" or "flanken" ribs and can usually be found at your butcher's counter.

Mexican-Style Pork Sandwich

HANDS-ON TIME	TOTAL TIME	MAKES
30 MINUTES	1½ HOURS	4 SERVINGS

2 tbsp	lime juice
1	canned chipotle pepper in adobo sauce, finely chopped
1 tsp	adobo sauce
½ tsp	dried oregano
¼ tsp	each ground cumin, ground coriander, salt and pepper
1	pork tenderloin (about 450 g), sliced ¼ inch (5 mm) thick
1	avocado, peeled, pitted and chopped
2 tbsp	chopped fresh cilantro
4	round challah buns or sesame hamburger buns
8	leaves Boston lettuce
2	small tomatoes, thinly sliced
½ cup	thinly sliced red onion

In bowl, combine half of the lime juice, the chipotle pepper, adobo sauce, oregano, cumin, coriander, salt and pepper. Add pork, turning to coat. Cover and refrigerate for 1 hour. *(Make-ahead: Refrigerate for up to 24 hours.)*

In bowl, mash avocado with fork; mix in cilantro and remaining lime juice. Set aside.

Weave pork slices onto 4 metal or soaked wooden skewers. Place on greased grill over medium-high heat; close lid and grill, turning occasionally, until juices run clear when pork is pierced and just a hint of pink remains inside, 8 to 10 minutes. Remove from skewers.

Layer bottom half of each bun with lettuce, tomatoes, pork, red onion and avocado mixture; sandwich layers with top half of bun.

NUTRITIONAL INFORMATION, PER SERVING: about 453 cal, 34 g pro, 15 g total fat (3 g sat. fat), 46 g carb (6 g dietary fibre, 4 g sugar), 101 mg chol, 620 mg sodium, 868 mg potassium. % RDI: 10% calcium, 31% iron, 15% vit A, 25% vit C, 56% folate.

TIP FROM THE TEST KITCHEN
Cemitas, as these sandwiches are known in Mexico, are often topped with Oaxacan-style stringy cheese. If you like, pull string cheese into thin strands and pile on top.

Hoisin Pork Tenderloin
WITH SESAME SOBA NOODLES

HANDS-ON TIME	TOTAL TIME	MAKES
30 MINUTES	30 MINUTES	4 SERVINGS

PORK Whisk together hoisin sauce, vinegar, sesame oil and chili sauce; set aside.

Place pork on greased grill over medium-high heat; close lid and grill, turning once, until juices run clear when pork is pierced and just a hint of pink remains inside, 16 to 20 minutes. Transfer to cutting board; tent with foil and let stand for 5 minutes. Brush pork with hoisin mixture and slice crosswise.

SESAME SOBA NOODLES While pork is cooking, halve bok choy lengthwise and remove core; brush bok choy all over with 1 tsp of the vegetable oil. Place on greased grill over medium-high heat; close lid and grill, turning once, until tender-crisp, about 4 minutes. Transfer to cutting board and let cool slightly; thinly slice crosswise.

In saucepan of boiling water, cook noodles according to package instructions. Drain and rinse under cold water; drain well.

In large bowl, whisk together vinegar, sesame seeds, soy sauce, sesame oil, mustard and remaining vegetable oil. Add noodles, bok choy, three-quarters of the green onions and the carrots; toss to coat. Top with pork and remaining green onions.

NUTRITIONAL INFORMATION, PER SERVING: about 437 cal, 37 g pro, 12 g total fat (2 g sat. fat), 49 g carb (4 g dietary fibre, 4 g sugar), 61 mg chol, 402 mg sodium, 821 mg potassium. % RDI: 9% calcium, 24% iron, 74% vit A, 35% vit C, 27% folate.

PORK

1 tbsp	hoisin sauce
1 tsp	rice vinegar
1 tsp	sesame oil
½ tsp	Asian chili sauce (such as sriracha)
1	pork tenderloin (about 450 g), trimmed

SESAME SOBA NOODLES

2	heads baby bok choy (about 250 g total)
4 tsp	vegetable oil
225 g	soba noodles
1 tbsp	rice vinegar
1 tbsp	sesame seeds, toasted
2 tsp	sodium-reduced soy sauce
2 tsp	sesame oil
1 tsp	Dijon mustard
4	green onions, sliced
1 cup	julienned carrots

TIP FROM THE TEST KITCHEN

Add the noodles to the dressing just before serving; if you add them too early, they'll soak up too much of the liquid and become mushy.

Lemon Mint Pork Tenderloin

HANDS-ON TIME	TOTAL TIME	MAKES
15 MINUTES	35 MINUTES	4 TO 6 SERVINGS

1 tbsp	grated lemon zest
3 tbsp	lemon juice
3 tbsp	olive oil
3 tbsp	liquid honey
1 tbsp	chopped fresh mint
1	clove garlic, minced
2	pork tenderloins (each about 375 g), trimmed
¼ tsp	each salt and pepper

In large bowl, whisk together lemon zest and juice, oil, honey, mint and garlic. Add pork, turning to coat; cover and refrigerate for 10 minutes. *(Make-ahead: Refrigerate for up to 8 hours.)*

Place pork on greased grill over medium-high heat; brush with any remaining marinade. Close lid and grill, turning once, until juices run clear when pork is pierced and just a hint of pink remains inside, 15 to 20 minutes.

Transfer to cutting board and tent with foil; let stand for 5 minutes before carving into ½-inch thick slices. Sprinkle with salt and pepper.

NUTRITIONAL INFORMATION, PER EACH OF 6 SERVINGS: about 222 cal, 25 g pro, 9 g total fat (2 g sat. fat), 10 g carb (trace dietary fibre), 61 mg chol, 148 mg sodium, 375 mg potassium. % RDI: 1% calcium, 9% iron, 8% vit C, 3% folate.

VARIATION
Marmalade-Glazed Pork Tenderloin
Replace lemon marinade with 2 tbsp cider vinegar, 1 tbsp vegetable oil, 1 tbsp Dijon mustard, 2 tsp chopped fresh thyme and ¼ tsp each salt and pepper. Add pork, turning to coat; cover and refrigerate for 2 hours. *(Make-ahead: Refrigerate for up to 8 hours.)*

Grill pork as directed. In last minute of cooking, brush pork with 2 tbsp orange marmalade, turning until marmalade is slightly caramelized.

Peach-Chipotle Pork Tenderloin
WITH GRILLED ASPARAGUS

HANDS-ON TIME	TOTAL TIME	MAKES
15 MINUTES	30 MINUTES	4 SERVINGS

In small saucepan, bring jam, vinegar, garlic and chipotle peppers to boil over medium-high heat; cook, stirring occasionally, until jam is melted, about 2 minutes. Remove 2 tbsp glaze and set aside.

Sprinkle pork with pinch each of the salt and pepper; brush all over with glaze. Place on greased grill over medium-high heat; close lid and grill, turning occasionally, until instant-read thermometer inserted in centre reads 160°F, about 18 minutes. Let stand for 5 minutes before carving. Drizzle reserved glaze over top.

Meanwhile, toss together asparagus, oil and remaining salt and pepper. Add to grill and cook, turning occasionally, until tender-crisp, about 7 minutes. Serve with pork.

NUTRITIONAL INFORMATION, PER SERVING: about 250 cal, 26 g pro, 6 g total fat (2 g sat. fat), 22 g carb (1 g dietary fibre, 14 g sugar), 61 mg chol, 253 mg sodium, 486 mg potassium. % RDI: 3% calcium, 14% iron, 8% vit A, 12% vit C, 34% folate.

⅓ **cup**	peach jam
3 tbsp	white wine vinegar
2	cloves garlic, chopped
2	canned chipotle peppers in adobo sauce, drained, seeded and chopped
1	pork tenderloin (450 g), trimmed
¼ **tsp**	each salt and pepper
1	small bunch asparagus (about 250 g), trimmed
1 tbsp	olive oil

VARIATION
Raspberry-Chipotle Chicken With Grilled Asparagus
Replace peach jam with seedless raspberry jam; replace pork with 4 small boneless skinless chicken breasts. Grill chicken, turning once, until no longer pink inside, about 12 minutes.

Grilled Jerk Chicken Wings

HANDS-ON TIME	TOTAL TIME	MAKES
25 MINUTES	3 HOURS	ABOUT 24 WINGS

4	green onions, chopped
2 tbsp	lime juice
1 tbsp	sodium-reduced soy sauce
1 tbsp	vegetable oil
1	jalapeño pepper, seeded and chopped
2	cloves garlic, chopped
1 tbsp	chopped fresh thyme
2 tsp	ground allspice
1 tsp	each salt and packed brown sugar
½ tsp	each ground ginger and pepper
¼ tsp	each cinnamon and nutmeg
900 g	chicken wings and/or drumettes

In food processor, purée together green onions, lime juice, soy sauce, oil, jalapeño pepper, garlic, thyme, allspice, salt, brown sugar, ginger, pepper, cinnamon and nutmeg until smooth. Scrape into large bowl; add wings and toss to coat. Cover and refrigerate for 2 hours. *(Make-ahead: Refrigerate for up to 24 hours.)*

Place wings on greased rack set over foil-lined rimmed baking sheet. Bake in 350°F oven until juices run clear when thickest part is pierced, about 30 minutes. *(Make-ahead: Refrigerate in airtight container for up to 24 hours. Reheat on grill over medium heat before continuing.)*

Place wings on greased grill over medium-high heat; close lid and grill, turning once, until browned and crisp, 6 to 8 minutes.

NUTRITIONAL INFORMATION, PER WING: about 63 cal, 5 g pro, 4 g total fat (1 g sat. fat), 1 g carb (trace dietary fibre, trace sugar), 16 mg chol, 137 mg sodium, 50 mg potassium. % RDI: 1% calcium, 3% iron, 1% vit A, 2% vit C, 1% folate.

TIP FROM THE TEST KITCHEN
For low-stress entertaining, roast the wings the night before. Finish them on the grill when your guests arrive.

GRILLED JERK CHICKEN WINGS (OPPOSITE)
AND **BACON AND FETA MINI PIZZAS** (P.132)

Spiced Chicken
WITH TOMATO KABOBS

HANDS-ON TIME	TOTAL TIME	MAKES
15 MINUTES	40 MINUTES	4 SERVINGS

In shallow dish, combine yogurt, 1 tbsp of the lemon juice, the ginger, tomato paste, garlic, 1½ tsp of the garam masala and ¼ tsp of the salt. Add chicken and toss to coat; let stand for 15 minutes. *(Make-ahead: Cover and refrigerate for up to 24 hours.)*

Meanwhile, combine oil and remaining lemon juice, garam masala and salt; set aside. Alternately thread tomatoes and red onion onto metal skewers.

Place chicken on greased grill over medium-high heat; close lid and grill, turning halfway through, until juices run clear when thickest part is pierced, about 10 minutes.

Meanwhile, add skewers; grill, turning 4 times and brushing with oil mixture, until onion is slightly softened and tomatoes are slightly charred, about 4 minutes. Serve with chicken.

NUTRITIONAL INFORMATION, PER SERVING: about 222 cal, 23 g pro, 10 g total fat (2 g sat. fat), 10 g carb (2 g dietary fibre, 5 g sugar), 81 mg chol, 383 mg sodium, 546 mg potassium. % RDI: 6% calcium, 14% iron, 9% vit A, 23% vit C, 10% folate.

¼ cup	2% plain yogurt
2 tbsp	lemon juice
1 tbsp	grated fresh ginger
1 tbsp	tomato paste
2	cloves garlic, grated
2 tsp	garam masala
½ tsp	salt
450 g	boneless skinless chicken thighs
1 tbsp	olive oil
2 cups	cherry tomatoes
half	red onion, cut in ¾-inch chunks

TIP FROM THE TEST KITCHEN

Chicken thighs are a Test Kitchen favourite for grilling. They're far more forgiving than chicken breasts—thighs stay moist even if overcooked slightly.

Moroccan Chicken
WITH SPICED VEGETABLES

HANDS-ON TIME 30 MINUTES	TOTAL TIME 2¾ HOURS	MAKES 4 SERVINGS

MOROCCAN CHICKEN

⅓ cup	Greek yogurt
1 tbsp	each tahini and lemon juice
2	cloves garlic, minced
2 tsp	minced fresh ginger
1 tsp	ground coriander
½ tsp	ground cumin
¼ tsp	cinnamon
pinch	each salt and pepper
450 g	boneless skinless chicken breasts

SPICED VEGETABLES

2 tbsp	each lemon juice and olive oil
1	clove garlic, minced
1 tsp	minced fresh ginger
¼ tsp	each salt and pepper
pinch	cinnamon
1	small red onion, cut in ½-inch thick rounds
2	portobello mushrooms, stems and gills removed
1	zucchini, cut lengthwise in ½-inch thick slices
1	sweet red pepper, seeded and quartered
2 tbsp	chopped fresh cilantro

MOROCCAN CHICKEN In large bowl, combine yogurt, tahini, lemon juice, garlic, ginger, coriander, cumin, cinnamon, salt and pepper. Add chicken; toss to coat. Cover and refrigerate for 2 hours. *(Make-ahead: Refrigerate for up to 24 hours.)*

Place chicken on greased grill over medium-high heat; close lid and grill, turning occasionally, until no longer pink inside, about 8 minutes. Let stand for 3 minutes before slicing.

SPICED VEGETABLES Whisk together lemon juice, oil, garlic, ginger, salt, pepper and cinnamon.

Thread red onion rounds onto metal or soaked wooden skewers. Place red onion, mushrooms, zucchini and red pepper on greased grill over medium-high heat; close lid and grill, basting frequently with lemon mixture, until tender, about 7 minutes. Cut mushrooms in half. Place on platter along with remaining grilled vegetables; sprinkle with cilantro. Serve with sliced chicken.

NUTRITIONAL INFORMATION, PER SERVING: about 288 cal, 31 g pro, 13 g total fat (3 g sat. fat), 14 g carb (4 g dietary fibre, 5 g sugar), 74 mg chol, 229 mg sodium, 946 mg potassium. % RDI: 8% calcium, 13% iron, 14% vit A, 92% vit C, 17% folate.

TIP FROM THE TEST KITCHEN
Thread onion slices on skewers—lollipop style—to keep the smaller pieces from falling through the grill grate.

Lemon & Herb Spatchcock Chicken

HANDS-ON TIME	TOTAL TIME	MAKES
25 MINUTES	1½ HOURS	4 TO 6 SERVINGS

Stir together half of the oil, the lemon zest, parsley, garlic, thyme, tarragon, salt and pepper; set aside.

Using kitchen shears, cut chicken along each side of backbone; discard backbone. Turn chicken breast side up; press firmly on breastbone to flatten.

Gently loosen skin from breast meat, being careful not to tear skin. Spread lemon zest mixture under skin, covering breast and legs evenly. (*Make-ahead: Cover and refrigerate for up to 24 hours.*)

Set foil drip pan under 1 rack of 2-burner barbecue or under centre rack of 3-burner barbecue. Heat remaining burner(s) to medium-high heat (about 375°F). Brush skin side of chicken with remaining oil. Place chicken, skin side up, on greased grill over drip pan; close lid and grill, turning once, until juices run clear when chicken is pierced and instant-read thermometer inserted in thickest part of thigh reads 185°F, about 1 hour.

Transfer to cutting board; let stand for 10 minutes before carving.

2 tbsp	olive oil
1 tbsp	grated lemon zest
1 tbsp	chopped fresh parsley
2	cloves garlic, finely grated or pressed
1 tsp	chopped fresh thyme
1 tsp	chopped fresh tarragon
¼ tsp	each salt and pepper
1	whole chicken (1.5 kg)

NUTRITIONAL INFORMATION, PER EACH OF 6 SERVINGS: about 371 cal, 38 g pro, 23 g total fat (6 g sat. fat), 1 g carb (trace dietary fibre, trace sugar), 121 mg chol, 209 mg sodium, 319 mg potassium. % RDI: 2% calcium, 14% iron, 7% vit A, 3% vit C, 4% folate.

TIP FROM THE TEST KITCHEN
Barbecue temperatures vary, and the gauge on the lid can be inaccurate. For best results, place an oven thermometer in the grill chamber and adjust the heat as needed to reach the desired temperature.

Honey-Glazed Chicken & Balsamic Radicchio

HANDS-ON TIME	TOTAL TIME	MAKES
15 MINUTES	20 MINUTES	4 SERVINGS

2 tbsp	liquid honey
1 tbsp	grainy mustard
¼ tsp	each salt and pepper
450 g	boneless skinless chicken breasts
2 heads	radicchio
2 tbsp	balsamic vinegar
2 tbsp	extra-virgin olive oil
⅓ cup	crumbled goat cheese
1 tbsp	chopped fresh chives

Stir together honey, mustard and half each of the salt and pepper; set aside.

Place chicken on greased grill over medium heat; close lid and grill, turning once, until browned, about 8 minutes. Brush with half of the honey mixture. Close lid and continue grilling, turning and brushing frequently with honey mixture, until no longer pink inside, about 7 minutes. Transfer to cutting board and tent with foil; let stand for 5 minutes before slicing.

Meanwhile, keeping root end intact, cut each radicchio into 4 wedges. Whisk together vinegar, oil and remaining salt and pepper; drizzle over radicchio.

Place on grill over medium heat; close lid and grill, turning once, until lightly browned, 3 to 4 minutes. Transfer to platter; top with goat cheese and chives. Serve with sliced chicken.

NUTRITIONAL INFORMATION, PER SERVING: about 303 cal, 31 g pro, 13 g total fat (4 g sat. fat), 15 g carb (1 g dietary fibre, 11 g sugar), 76 mg chol, 349 mg sodium, 606 mg potassium. % RDI: 5% calcium, 11% iron, 7% vit A, 10% vit C, 20% folate.

TIP FROM THE TEST KITCHEN

Grilling radicchio mellows its slight bitterness, adds smoky flavour and softens its crunch. Serve it alongside grilled meats, as here, or use it as a tasty and surprising addition to salads and slaws.

Harissa Chicken
WITH SPICED FARRO

HANDS-ON TIME	TOTAL TIME	MAKES
30 MINUTES	30 MINUTES	4 SERVINGS

SPICED FARRO In saucepan of lightly salted boiling water, cook farro until tender yet still slightly firm, 20 to 25 minutes; drain. In large bowl, whisk together oil, lemon juice, harissa, paprika, salt and pepper. Stir in farro, chives and cilantro.

HARISSA CHICKEN While farro is cooking, in small bowl, whisk together honey, harissa, vinegar, garlic and half each of the salt and pepper; set aside.

Halve and core red pepper; cut each half into thirds. Toss with oil and remaining salt and pepper.

Place chicken on greased grill over medium-high heat; close lid and grill for 5 minutes. Turn chicken, brushing all over with half of the honey mixture. Close lid and grill until no longer pink inside, about 4 minutes.

While chicken is grilling, place red pepper on greased grill over medium-high heat; close lid and grill, turning once, until tender, 7 to 8 minutes.

Turn chicken and red pepper; brush chicken with remaining honey mixture. Close lid and grill for 1 minute. Serve with farro.

NUTRITIONAL INFORMATION, PER SERVING: about 452 cal, 32 g pro, 14 g total fat (2 g sat. fat), 49 g carb (6 g dietary fibre, 11 g sugar), 66 mg chol, 397 mg sodium, 622 mg potassium. % RDI: 4% calcium, 17% iron, 21% vit A, 135% vit C, 7% folate.

SPICED FARRO
1 cup	farro, rinsed
2 tbsp	olive oil
1 tbsp	lemon juice
1 tsp	harissa paste
¼ tsp	each paprika, salt and pepper
¼ cup	each chopped fresh chives and fresh cilantro

HARISSA CHICKEN
2 tbsp	liquid honey
1 tbsp	harissa paste
1 tsp	red wine vinegar
3	cloves garlic, finely grated or pressed
¼ tsp	each salt and pepper
1	sweet red pepper
2 tsp	olive oil
2	large boneless skinless chicken breasts (about 450 g total), halved horizontally

TIP FROM THE TEST KITCHEN
No farro in the cupboard? Substitute another whole grain, such as barley, wild rice, or spelt, cooked according to the package directions.

Chicken Cutlets
WITH CILANTRO PEANUT SAUCE

HANDS-ON TIME	TOTAL TIME	MAKES
30 MINUTES	35 MINUTES	4 SERVINGS

1½ cups	packed fresh parsley leaves
½ cup	packed fresh cilantro leaves
⅓ cup	chopped roasted peanuts
¼ cup	peanut oil or vegetable oil
2½ tbsp	white wine vinegar
½ tsp	each salt and pepper
4	boneless skinless chicken breasts (about 450 g total)

Finely chop parsley and cilantro; scrape into bowl. Stir in peanuts, all but 2 tsp of the oil, the vinegar and half each of the salt and pepper. Set aside. *(Make-ahead: Refrigerate in airtight container for up to 2 days.)*

Between plastic wrap, use meat mallet or bottom of heavy pan to flatten chicken to ¼-inch (5 mm) thickness. Brush with remaining oil; sprinkle with remaining salt and pepper.

Place chicken on greased grill over medium-high heat; close lid and grill, turning once, until chicken is no longer pink inside, about 5 minutes. Spoon sauce over chicken before serving.

NUTRITIONAL INFORMATION, PER SERVING: about 347 cal, 34 g pro, 22 g total fat (4 g sat. fat), 4 g carb (2 g dietary fibre), 79 mg chol, 422 mg sodium, 597 mg potassium. % RDI: 5% calcium, 16% iron, 21% vit A, 52% vit C, 25% folate.

TIP FROM THE TEST KITCHEN
Try Cilantro Peanut Sauce with grilled pork chops or tenderloin.

Pomegranate-Glazed Cornish Hens

HANDS-ON TIME	TOTAL TIME	MAKES
20 MINUTES	50 MINUTES	8 SERVINGS

POMEGRANATE GLAZE In saucepan, bring pomegranate juice and vinegar to boil; boil until reduced to ⅓ cup, about 10 minutes. Stir in honey and cinnamon; let cool slightly. *(Make-ahead: Refrigerate in airtight container for up to 1 week.)*

CORNISH HENS Using kitchen shears, cut 1 hen down each side of backbone; discard backbone or reserve for another use. Cut 1 hen in half lengthwise through breastbone. Trim excess fat and skin. Repeat with remaining hens. Sprinkle with salt and pepper.

Heat 1 burner of 2-burner barbecue or 2 outside burners of 3-burner barbecue to medium heat. Place hens, bone side down, over unlit burner on greased grill. Close lid and grill until bottom is marked, about 25 minutes.

Brush with half of the pomegranate glaze; turn and brush with remaining glaze. Grill until juices run clear when thighs are pierced, about 20 minutes. Move any pieces that need more crisping or colouring over lit burner. Close lid and grill until golden brown, about 3 minutes.

NUTRITIONAL INFORMATION, PER SERVING: about 159 cal, 23 g pro, 4 g total fat (1 g sat. fat), 7 g carb (trace dietary fibre), 104 mg chol, 137 mg sodium. % RDI: 2% calcium, 6% iron, 2% vit A, 2% vit C, 1% folate.

VARIATION
Teriyaki-Glazed Cornish Hens
Replace pomegranate glaze with teriyaki sauce, page 116.

POMEGRANATE GLAZE

1 cup	pomegranate juice
2 tbsp	balsamic vinegar
1½ tsp	liquid honey
¼ tsp	cinnamon

CORNISH HENS

4	Cornish hens
¼ tsp	each salt and pepper

Grilled Rosemary Mustard Chicken

HANDS-ON TIME 15 MINUTES	TOTAL TIME 25 MINUTES	MAKES 4 SERVINGS

1½ tsp	grainy mustard
1½ tsp	Dijon mustard
1½ tsp	lemon juice
1 tsp	liquid honey
¾ tsp	chopped fresh rosemary
450 g	boneless skinless chicken thighs
pinch	each salt and pepper

Whisk together grainy and Dijon mustards, lemon juice, honey and rosemary; set aside.

Sprinkle chicken with salt and pepper. Place on greased grill over medium-high heat; close lid and grill, turning once, for 8 minutes. Brush with mustard mixture; cook, turning once, until juices run clear when thickest part is pierced, about 2 minutes. Let stand for 5 minutes before serving.

NUTRITIONAL INFORMATION, PER SERVING: about 154 cal, 22 g pro, 6 g total fat (2 g sat. fat), 2 g carb (0 g dietary fibre, 2 g sugar), 94 mg chol, 146 mg sodium, 270 mg potassium. %RDI: 2% calcium, 9% iron, 2% vit A, 5% vit C, 3% folate.

TIP FROM THE TEST KITCHEN
Wind, rain and cool weather can affect the temperature inside the barbecue, but bad weather shouldn't stop you from grilling. You may need to give your meal a little more time on the grill or turn up the heat to compensate.

Maple Buttermilk Grilled Chicken

HANDS-ON TIME	TOTAL TIME	MAKES
45 MINUTES	2¾ HOURS	10 TO 12 SERVINGS

In large bowl, combine buttermilk, green onions, garlic, pepper, cinnamon and hot pepper flakes. Add chicken, turning to coat. Cover and refrigerate for 2 hours. *(Make-ahead: Refrigerate for up to 24 hours.)*

Remove chicken from marinade; discard marinade. Sprinkle chicken with salt. Place on greased grill over medium-high heat; close lid and grill, turning occasionally, until juices run clear when thickest part is pierced, about 35 minutes.

Continue grilling, brushing with maple syrup, until glossy and coated, about 5 minutes.

NUTRITIONAL INFORMATION, PER EACH OF 12 SERVINGS: about 113 cal, 10 g pro, 5 g total fat (2 g sat. fat), 6 g carb (trace dietary fibre, 5 g sugar), 34 mg chol, 149 mg sodium, 157 mg potassium. % RDI: 3% calcium, 2% iron, 2% vit A, 2% folate.

2 cups	buttermilk
2	green onions, chopped
4	cloves garlic, minced
½ tsp	pepper
¼ tsp	each cinnamon and hot pepper flakes
20	small bone-in skin-on chicken pieces (about 2.5 kg total)
½ tsp	salt
¼ cup	maple syrup

TIP FROM THE TEST KITCHEN

To separate chicken legs into thighs and drumsticks, look for a thin line of fat at the joint. With a sharp knife, cut along that line and through the joint. Cut whole chicken breasts in half, through the bone, so they're similar in size to the other pieces.

Chicken Tikka Salad

HANDS-ON TIME	TOTAL TIME	MAKES
35 MINUTES	35 MINUTES	4 TO 6 SERVINGS

SPICED LEMON DRESSING

¼ cup	lemon juice
4 tsp	liquid honey
1 tbsp	Dijon mustard
1 tbsp	grated fresh ginger
1	clove garlic, finely grated or pressed
½ tsp	garam masala
¼ tsp	each salt and pepper
½ cup	vegetable oil

SALAD

¼ cup	plain Balkan-style yogurt
2 tsp	each garam masala and sweet paprika
¼ tsp	each salt and pepper
pinch	cayenne pepper
450 g	boneless skinless chicken breast cutlets
2	sweet red, yellow and/or orange peppers, quartered
1	large red onion, cut crosswise in ½-inch rings
1	naan
2 tsp	vegetable oil
16 cups	chopped romaine lettuce

SPICED LEMON DRESSING In small bowl, whisk together lemon juice, honey, mustard, ginger, garlic, garam masala, salt and pepper. Slowly whisk in oil. Set aside. *(Make-ahead: Refrigerate in airtight container for up to 5 days. Let stand at room temperature for 30 minutes and whisk before serving.)*

SALAD In large bowl, stir together yogurt, garam masala, paprika, salt, pepper and cayenne pepper. Add chicken, turning to coat. *(Make-ahead: Cover and refrigerate for up to 24 hours.)*

In separate bowl, toss together sweet peppers, red onion and ¼ cup of the dressing; reserve remaining dressing.

Place chicken on greased grill over medium-high heat. Reserving excess dressing from bowl, transfer sweet peppers and red onion to grill. Close lid and grill, turning chicken and vegetables once and brushing vegetables with reserved dressing from bowl, until chicken is no longer pink inside and vegetables are tender, about 10 minutes.

Transfer chicken and vegetables to cutting board; tent with foil. Let stand for 5 minutes.

While chicken is standing, brush both sides of naan with oil; place on greased grill over medium-high heat. Grill, turning once, just until crisp, about 5 minutes.

Chop chicken, sweet peppers, red onion and naan into bite-size pieces. In separate large bowl, combine chicken, sweet peppers, red onion, naan, lettuce and remaining dressing; toss to coat.

NUTRITIONAL INFORMATION, PER EACH OF 6 SERVINGS: about 399 cal, 22 g pro, 24 g total fat (3 g sat. fat), 26 g carb (5 g dietary fibre, 10 g sugar), 45 mg chol, 424 mg sodium, 628 mg potassium. % RDI: 6% calcium, 18% iron, 97% vit A, 195% vit C, 62% folate.

Napa Cabbage Slaw
WITH GRILLED CHICKEN

HANDS-ON TIME	TOTAL TIME	MAKES
20 MINUTES	30 MINUTES	4 SERVINGS

SOY VINAIGRETTE Whisk together vegetable oil, vinegar, soy sauce, sesame oil and salt; set aside.

SALAD Sprinkle chicken with salt and pepper. Place on greased grill over medium-high heat; close lid and grill, turning once, until no longer pink inside, 12 to 15 minutes. Let stand for 5 minutes before slicing.

In large bowl, add cabbage, carrot, red pepper, celery, cucumber, green onions and vinaigrette; toss to coat. Top with chicken; sprinkle with almonds.

NUTRITIONAL INFORMATION, PER SERVING: about 293 cal, 30 g pro, 15 g total fat (2 g sat. fat), 11 g carb (3 g dietary fibre, 5 g sugar), 67 mg chol, 242 mg sodium, 786 mg potassium. % RDI: 10% calcium, 11% iron, 40% vit A, 123% vit C, 39% folate.

VARIATION
Creamy Tahini Slaw With Grilled Chicken
Replace soy vinaigrette with 2 tbsp olive oil, 4 tsp lemon juice, 1 tbsp tahini, 1 tbsp Balkan-style plain yogurt and ¼ tsp each salt and pepper.

SOY VINAIGRETTE

2 tbsp	vegetable oil
4 tsp	unseasoned rice vinegar
1 tbsp	sodium-reduced soy sauce
2 tsp	sesame oil
pinch	salt

SALAD

450 g	boneless skinless chicken breasts
pinch	each salt and pepper
4 cups	lightly packed shredded napa cabbage
1	carrot, julienned or grated
1	sweet red pepper, thinly sliced
1	rib celery, thinly sliced diagonally
half	English cucumber, halved lengthwise, seeded and thinly sliced diagonally
2	green onions, thinly sliced
⅓ cup	sliced almonds, toasted

Turkey Cutlets
WITH FRESH SAGE

HANDS-ON TIME	TOTAL TIME	MAKES
5 MINUTES	2¼ HOURS	4 SERVINGS

¼ cup	olive oil
3	cloves garlic, minced
2 tbsp	minced fresh sage
½ tsp	salt
¼ tsp	pepper
450 g	turkey or chicken cutlets or scaloppine

In shallow bowl, whisk together oil, garlic, sage, salt and pepper. Add turkey, turning to coat. Cover and refrigerate for 2 hours. *(Make-ahead: Refrigerate for up to 4 hours.)*

Place on greased grill over medium-high heat; brush with remaining marinade. Close lid and grill, turning once, until no longer pink inside, about 6 minutes.

NUTRITIONAL INFORMATION, PER SERVING: about 245 cal, 27 g pro, 14 g total fat (2 g sat. fat), 1 g carb (trace dietary fibre), 74 mg chol, 334 mg sodium. % RDI: 2% calcium, 11% iron, 2% vit C, 2% folate.

TIP FROM THE TEST KITCHEN
Buy turkey cutlets or make your own by cutting a single turkey breast crosswise into 1-inch thick slices. Pound slices to ½-inch thickness.

MARINADES

Lemon, Herb & Garlic Marinade

HANDS-ON TIME 10 MINUTES
TOTAL TIME 10 MINUTES
MAKES ABOUT ¾ CUP

⅓ cup	olive oil
¼ cup	white wine vinegar
2 tbsp	each chopped fresh thyme and fresh oregano
4 tsp	grated lemon zest
2 tbsp	lemon juice
4	cloves garlic, minced
1 tsp	each salt and pepper

Whisk together oil, vinegar, thyme, oregano, lemon zest, lemon juice, garlic, salt and pepper.

NUTRITIONAL INFORMATION, PER 2 TBSP: about 116 cal, trace pro, 12 g total fat (2 g sat. fat), 2 g carb (1 g dietary fibre, trace sugar), 0 mg chol, 384 mg sodium, 38 mg potassium. % RDI: 2% calcium, 4% iron, 1% vit A, 10% vit C, 1% folate.

Apple Cider & Shallot Marinade

HANDS-ON TIME 10 MINUTES
TOTAL TIME 10 MINUTES
MAKES ABOUT 1 CUP

¾ cup	apple cider or apple juice
2 tbsp	cider vinegar
4	shallots, sliced
3	sprigs fresh thyme
1 tsp	whole allspice
1 tsp	Dijon mustard
½ tsp	Worcestershire sauce

Whisk together cider, vinegar, shallots, thyme, allspice, mustard and Worcestershire sauce.

NUTRITIONAL INFORMATION, PER 2 TBSP: about 17 cal, trace pro, trace total fat (0 g sat. fat), 5 g carb (trace dietary fibre, 3 g sugar), 0 mg chol, 13 mg sodium, 55 mg potassium. % RDI: 1% calcium, 2% iron, 1% vit A, 2% vit C, 1% folate.

Tandoori Yogurt Marinade

HANDS-ON TIME 10 MINUTES
TOTAL TIME 10 MINUTES
MAKES ABOUT 1 CUP

¾ cup	2% plain yogurt
2 tbsp	chopped fresh cilantro
2 tbsp	lemon juice
1	clove garlic, minced
1 tbsp	grated fresh ginger
1 tbsp	garam masala
1 tsp	paprika
1 tsp	salt
1 tsp	cracked pepper

Whisk together yogurt, cilantro, lemon juice, garlic, ginger, garam masala, paprika, salt and pepper.

NUTRITIONAL INFORMATION, PER 2 TBSP: about 21 cal, 1 g pro, 1 g total fat (trace sat. fat), 3 g carb (trace dietary fibre, 1 g sugar), 2 mg chol, 304 mg sodium, 83 mg potassium. % RDI: 4% calcium, 3% iron, 2% vit A, 3% vit C.

HOW TO

For 4 servings—450 g boneless (or 675 g bone-in) meat or poultry, or 450 g fish—
use ½ cup marinade. Cover and refrigerate fish and seafood in marinade for no
more than 30 minutes. Marinate meat and poultry for 6 hours.
(Make-ahead: Cover and refrigerate meat or poultry for up to 24 hours.)

Cedar-Planked Salmon
WITH MAPLE-MUSTARD GLAZE

HANDS-ON TIME	TOTAL TIME	MAKES
10 MINUTES	50 MINUTES	6 SERVINGS

750 g	salmon fillet
¼ cup	maple syrup
2 tbsp	grainy Dijon mustard
½ tsp	salt
¼ tsp	pepper

Soak 12- × 7-inch untreated cedar plank in water for 30 minutes or for up to 24 hours; place fish on top.

In small bowl, whisk together maple syrup, mustard, salt and pepper; brush half over fish.

Place plank on grill over medium-high heat; close lid and grill, brushing fish once with remaining maple mixture, until fish flakes easily when tested, 20 to 25 minutes.

NUTRITIONAL INFORMATION, PER SERVING: about 222 cal, 20 g pro, 12 g total fat (2 g sat. fat), 10 g carb (trace dietary fibre), 56 mg chol, 314 mg sodium, 374 mg potassium. % RDI: 2% calcium, 4% iron, 2% vit A, 6% vit C, 14% folate.

TIP FROM THE TEST KITCHEN
Grilling a halved lemon adds a caramelized, smoky flavour to its juice—just brush the cut sides with a little vegetable oil and place on grill over medium-high heat until slightly charred, about 10 minutes.

Grilled Salmon & Couscous Pouches

HANDS-ON TIME	TOTAL TIME	MAKES
15 MINUTES	25 MINUTES	4 SERVINGS

In large bowl, stir together couscous, boiling water and butter. Let stand for 5 minutes. Stir in orange pepper, zucchini, tomato, 4 tsp of the pesto and ¼ tsp each of the salt and pepper.

Place four 16-inch lengths of heavy-duty foil (or double thickness of regular foil) on work surface. Arrange one 10-inch length of parchment paper in centre of each. Spoon about 1 cup of the couscous mixture onto centre of each. Top with fish. Sprinkle fish with remaining salt and pepper; spread remaining pesto over top. Bring together 2 opposite ends of foil and fold to seal, leaving room inside for expansion; fold in remaining sides to seal.

Place packets on grill over medium-high heat; close lid and grill until fish flakes easily when tested, about 15 minutes. Let stand for 2 minutes before serving.

NUTRITIONAL INFORMATION, PER SERVING: about 471 cal, 28 g pro, 28 g total fat (10 g sat. fat), 26 g carb (2 g dietary fibre, 3 g sugar), 85 mg chol, 525 mg sodium, 718 mg potassium. % RDI: 5% calcium, 9% iron, 22% vit A, 107% vit C, 15% folate.

⅔ cup	couscous
½ cup	boiling water
3 tbsp	butter, melted
1	sweet orange pepper, seeded and chopped
1	zucchini, chopped
1	ripe tomato, chopped
3 tbsp	prepared pesto
½ tsp	each salt and pepper
4	skinless salmon fillets, 1-inch thick (about 450 g total)

TIP FROM THE TEST KITCHEN
Folding the packets securely ensures an airtight seal. Open them carefully to ensure the steam doesn't burn your hands.

Pickerel & Potato Pouches

HANDS-ON TIME	TOTAL TIME	MAKES
15 MINUTES	25 MINUTES	4 SERVINGS

3 tbsp	olive oil
2 tbsp	lemon juice
1 tbsp	chopped fresh parsley
2 tsp	chopped fresh dill
½ tsp	each salt and pepper
340 g	yellow-fleshed potatoes (unpeeled), sliced paper-thin crosswise (about 1 large)
1	small onion, thinly sliced
675 g	skinless pickerel fillets, cut in 4 portions

Whisk together 2 tbsp of the oil, the lemon juice, parsley, dill and half each of the salt and pepper; set aside.

In bowl, toss together potatoes, onion and remaining oil, salt and pepper.

Place four 16-inch lengths of heavy-duty foil (or double thickness of regular foil) on work surface. Divide potato mixture among foil pieces. Top each with fish; drizzle with lemon mixture. Bring together 2 opposite ends of foil and fold to seal, leaving room inside for expansion; fold in remaining sides to seal.

Place packets on grill over medium-high heat; close lid and cook until potatoes are tender, 12 to 15 minutes.

NUTRITIONAL INFORMATION, PER SERVING: about 320 cal, 35 g pro, 12 g total fat (2 g sat. fat), 17 g carb (2 g dietary fibre), 146 mg chol, 383 mg sodium, 1,138 mg potassium. % RDI: 19% calcium, 26% iron, 4% vit A, 27% vit C, 11% folate.

(30)

TIP FROM THE TEST KITCHEN

Almost any mild-flavoured white fish (such as tilapia or halibut) can be used in this recipe instead of pickerel.

A mandoline is the best tool for cutting thin, uniform potato slices. If you don't have one, use cooked potatoes, cut into thicker slices.

Grilled Curry Shrimp Tacos

HANDS-ON TIME	TOTAL TIME	MAKES
15 MINUTES	30 MINUTES	4 SERVINGS

In large bowl, whisk together 3 tbsp of the oil, 2 tbsp of the lime juice, the ketchup, soy sauce, curry powder, garlic, half each of the salt and pepper, and the allspice. Add shrimp and toss to coat; set aside.

Brush sweet peppers and onion with 1 tbsp of the remaining oil. Place on greased grill over medium-high heat; close lid and grill, turning once, until tender, 10 to 12 minutes. Cut into chunks.

In food processor, coarsely chop grilled vegetables and jalapeño pepper; transfer to large bowl. Add cilantro and remaining oil, lime juice, salt and pepper; toss to combine. Set salsa aside.

Thread shrimp onto metal or soaked wooden skewers. Place on greased grill over medium-high heat; close lid and grill, turning once, until pink and opaque throughout, 4 to 5 minutes. Divide shrimp and salsa among tortillas.

NUTRITIONAL INFORMATION, PER SERVING: about 445 cal, 25 g pro, 18 g total fat (3 g sat. fat), 50 g carb (6 g dietary fibre), 129 mg chol, 664 mg sodium, 615 mg potassium. % RDI: 8% calcium, 31% iron, 28% vit A, 318% vit C, 23% folate.

⅓ cup	olive oil
¼ cup	lime juice
1 tbsp	ketchup
2 tsp	sodium-reduced soy sauce
1 tsp	curry powder
2	cloves garlic, minced
¼ tsp	each salt and pepper
pinch	ground allspice
450 g	raw jumbo shrimp (21 to 24 count), peeled, deveined and tail removed
2	each sweet red and yellow peppers, seeded and quartered
1	onion, cut in ½-inch thick rings
1	jalapeño pepper, seeded
¼ cup	chopped fresh cilantro
8	whole grain flour tortillas (6 inches)

TIP FROM THE TEST KITCHEN

If you prefer, warm the tortillas on the grill while the shrimp are cooking. Wrap the stacked tortillas in a double layer of foil; place on grill with shrimp until heated through, about 4 minutes.

Cajun Shrimp
WITH SUMMER VEGETABLE ORZO

HANDS-ON TIME 15 MINUTES	TOTAL TIME 20 MINUTES	MAKES 4 SERVINGS

CAJUN SHRIMP

450 g	jumbo shrimp (21 to 24 count), peeled and deveined
2	cloves garlic, minced
1 tbsp	lemon juice
1 tsp	Cajun seasoning
1 tsp	olive oil

SUMMER VEGETABLE ORZO

2	zucchini, cut lengthwise in ½-inch thick slices
2	corn cobs, husked
1	carrot, cut lengthwise in ¼-inch (5 mm) thick slices
2 tbsp	extra-virgin olive oil
1 cup	orzo
¼ cup	thinly sliced fresh basil
3 tbsp	lemon juice
½ tsp	pepper
¼ tsp	salt

CAJUN SHRIMP In bowl, toss together shrimp, garlic, lemon juice, Cajun seasoning and oil; let stand for 10 minutes.

Thread shrimp onto metal or soaked wooden skewers. Place on greased grill over medium-high heat; close lid and grill, turning once, until pink and opaque throughout, 4 to 5 minutes.

SUMMER VEGETABLE ORZO Meanwhile, toss together zucchini, corn cobs, carrot and half of the oil. Place vegetables on greased grill over medium-high heat; close lid and grill, turning occasionally, until tender, 10 to 12 minutes.

While vegetables are cooking, in saucepan of boiling salted water, cook orzo according to package directions; drain and transfer to large bowl.

Transfer vegetables to cutting board; chop zucchini and carrots. Cut kernels from corn cobs. Add vegetables to orzo along with remaining oil, the basil, lemon juice, pepper and salt; toss to coat. Serve with shrimp.

NUTRITIONAL INFORMATION, PER SERVING: about 410 cal, 26 g pro, 11 g total fat (2 g sat. fat), 54 g carb (6 g dietary fibre, 6 g sugar), 129 mg chol, 428 mg sodium, 639 mg potassium. % RDI: 7% calcium, 26% iron, 49% vit A, 23% vit C, 49% folate.

TIP FROM THE TEST KITCHEN

To make your own batch of Cajun seasoning, combine ¼ cup each sweet paprika and dried parsley; 2 tbsp each garlic powder, dried oregano and dried thyme; 1 tsp salt; and ½ tsp cayenne pepper. *(Make-ahead: Store in airtight container for up to 1 month.)*

Grilled Shrimp
WITH SRIRACHA-LIME COCKTAIL SAUCE

HANDS-ON TIME	TOTAL TIME	MAKES
15 MINUTES	15 MINUTES	12 SERVINGS

COCKTAIL SAUCE Whisk together chili sauce, horseradish, lime juice, sriracha, salt and pepper; set aside. *(Make-ahead: Cover and refrigerate for up to 3 days.)*

SHRIMP In bowl, toss together shrimp, oil, salt and pepper. Thread shrimp onto metal or soaked wooden skewers. Place on greased grill over medium-high heat; close lid and grill, turning once, until pink and opaque throughout, 4 to 5 minutes. Serve with cocktail sauce.

NUTRITIONAL INFORMATION, PER SERVING: about 54 cal, 7 g pro, 1 g total fat (trace sat. fat), 4 g carb (1 g dietary fibre, 2 g sugar), 60 mg chol, 319 mg sodium, 126 mg potassium. % RDI: 1% calcium, 7% iron, 2% vit A, 3% vit C, 3% folate.

COCKTAIL SAUCE

¾ cup	tomato-based chili sauce or ketchup
2 tbsp	drained prepared horseradish
1 tbsp	each lime juice and sriracha
pinch	each salt and pepper

SHRIMP

450 g	jumbo shrimp (21 to 24 count), peeled (tail-on) and deveined
1 tsp	olive oil
pinch	each salt and pepper

TIP FROM THE TEST KITCHEN

As with any chili-spiced dish, adjust amounts to suit your guests' tastes. Tomato-based chili sauces are usually quite mild, but sriracha packs a punch.

Garlic & Herb Seafood Skewers

HANDS-ON TIME	TOTAL TIME	MAKES
30 MINUTES	30 MINUTES	4 SERVINGS

3 tbsp	chopped fresh chives
3 tbsp	olive oil
2 tbsp	lemon juice
1 tbsp	chopped fresh thyme
2	cloves garlic, minced
pinch	salt
¼ tsp	pepper
16	jumbo shrimp (21 to 24 count), peeled and deveined
225 g	firm white fish fillets, cut in ¾-inch pieces
1 cup	vegetable broth
⅔ cup	couscous
1 tbsp	grated lemon zest

In bowl, combine chives, oil, lemon juice, thyme, garlic, salt and pinch of the pepper. Add shrimp and fish; toss to coat.

In small saucepan, bring broth to boil; remove from heat. Stir in couscous, lemon zest and remaining pepper. Cover and let stand until no liquid remains, about 5 minutes. Fluff with fork.

Meanwhile, thread fish and shrimp onto metal skewers. Place on greased grill over medium-high heat; close lid and grill, turning once, until fish is opaque and shrimp are pink and opaque throughout, about 5 minutes. Serve over couscous.

NUTRITIONAL INFORMATION, PER SERVING: about 289 cal, 28 g pro, 9 g total fat (1 g sat. fat), 24 g carb (1 g dietary fibre, 1 g sugar), 129 mg chol, 331 mg sodium, 308 mg potassium. % RDI: 5% calcium, 17% iron, 6% vit A, 12% vit C, 12% folate.

TIP FROM THE TEST KITCHEN
Any firm-fleshed fish (such as cod, basa or tilapia) is perfect for these skewers. Cutting the fish into pieces about the same size as the shrimp ensures both cook in the same amount of time.

Mango Scallop Skewers
WITH SPINACH TOSS

HANDS-ON TIME	TOTAL TIME	MAKES
15 MINUTES	15 MINUTES	4 SERVINGS

SCALLOPS Alternately thread 3 scallops and 2 mango cubes onto each of 8 metal or soaked wooden skewers.

In small bowl, gradually whisk butter into mustard; brush half over 1 side of the skewers. Place, buttered side down, on greased grill over medium-high heat. Close lid and grill for 2 minutes. Brush with remaining butter mixture; turn and grill until scallops are opaque, about 2 minutes.

SPINACH TOSS Meanwhile, combine spinach, red pepper, mango and red onion; arrange on platter. Whisk together oil, lemon juice, mustard, salt and pepper; drizzle over salad. Top with skewers.

NUTRITIONAL INFORMATION, PER SERVING: about 249 cal, 17 g pro, 14 g total fat (5 g sat. fat), 16 g carb (3 g dietary fibre, 12 g sugar), 49 mg chol, 294 mg sodium, 735 mg potassium. % RDI: 12% calcium, 25% iron, 62% vit A, 108% vit C, 53% folate.

SCALLOPS

400 g	jumbo scallops (20 to 40 count)
1	mango, peeled, pitted and cut in sixteen ¾-inch cubes
2 tbsp	butter, melted
2 tsp	mustard

SPINACH TOSS

6 cups	baby spinach
1	sweet red pepper, julienned
⅓ cup	julienned peeled mango
¼ cup	thinly sliced red onion
2 tbsp	olive oil
2 tsp	lemon juice
1 tsp	Dijon mustard
pinch	each salt and pepper

TIP FROM THE TEST KITCHEN
Clean and grease the grates well before you grill fish and seafood; leftover food residue can cause sticking.

Bacon-Wrapped Beef Kabobs

HANDS-ON TIME	TOTAL TIME	MAKES
25 MINUTES	30 MINUTES	4 SERVINGS

4	strips bacon, halved lengthwise and cut crosswise in thirds
400 g	top sirloin grilling steak, cut in 1½-inch chunks
1	small sweet red pepper, seeded and cut in 1-inch pieces
half	red onion, cut in 1-inch pieces
8	large cremini mushrooms, stemmed and halved
2 tbsp	olive oil
1 tbsp	chopped fresh rosemary
1	clove garlic, minced
¼ tsp	each salt and pepper

Wrap 1 piece of bacon around each piece of steak, overlapping ends of bacon slightly. Alternately thread steak, red pepper, red onion and mushrooms onto metal or soaked wooden skewers, piercing both ends of each piece of bacon to secure.

Stir together oil, rosemary and garlic; brush onto skewers. Sprinkle with salt and pepper. Place on grill over medium-high heat; close lid and grill, turning occasionally, until steak is medium-rare, about 6 minutes. Let stand for 2 minutes before serving.

NUTRITIONAL INFORMATION, PER SERVING: about 259 cal, 24 g pro, 14 g total fat (4 g sat. fat), 8 g carb (2 g dietary fibre, 4 g sugar), 55 mg chol, 371 mg sodium, 595 mg potassium. % RDI: 2% calcium, 18% iron, 9% vit A, 82% vit C, 9% folate.

TIP FROM THE TEST KITCHEN
For best results, use hefty, flat metal skewers or wooden skewers for kabobs. Foods tend to spin on round metal skewers, making it difficult to cook kabobs evenly on all sides.

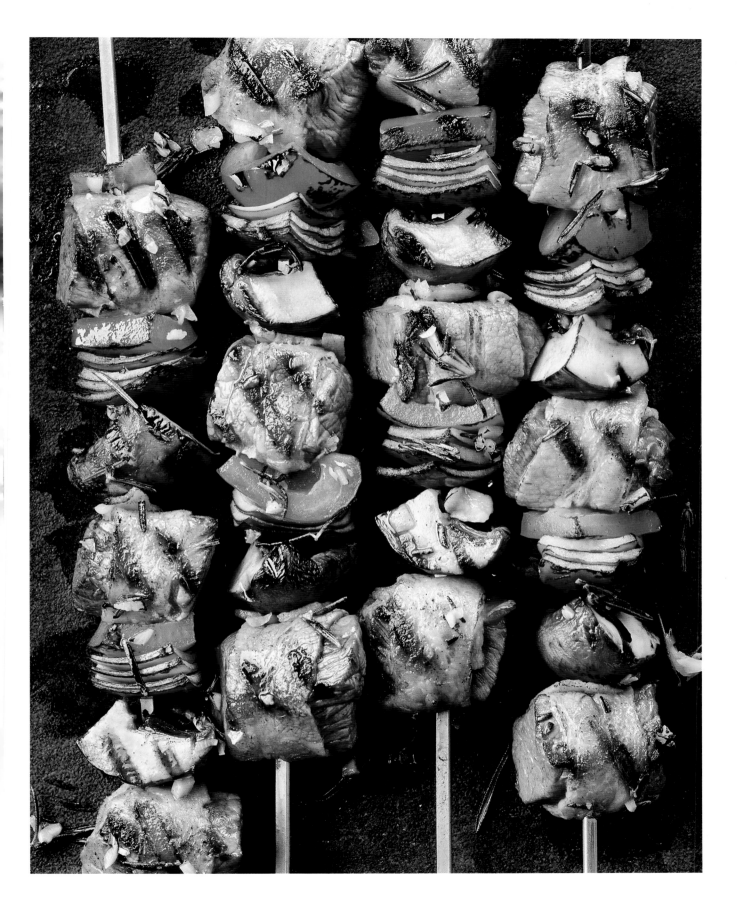

Spicy Adobo Beef Brochettes
WITH MELON CUCUMBER RELISH

HANDS-ON TIME 15 MINUTES	TOTAL TIME 25 MINUTES	MAKES 4 SERVINGS

BEEF BROCHETTES Trim fat from steak; cut steak into 1-inch cubes and place in bowl. Add adobo sauce, garlic, salt and pepper; toss to combine. Let stand for 10 minutes.

Cut ½ inch off top and bottom of red onion; finely dice top and bottom and set aside. Cut remaining onion into 1-inch chunks.

Alternately thread beef and onion chunks loosely onto metal or soaked wooden skewers. Place on greased grill over medium-high heat; close lid and grill, turning 3 times, until beef is browned but still pink inside, about 10 minutes.

MELON CUCUMBER RELISH Meanwhile, toss together melon, cucumber, parsley, vinegar, oil, sugar, salt, pepper and reserved diced onion. Serve with brochettes.

NUTRITIONAL INFORMATION, PER SERVING: about 263 cal, 24 g pro, 12 g total fat (3 g sat. fat), 15 g carb (2 g dietary fibre, 9 g sugar), 53 mg chol, 415 mg sodium, 528 mg potassium. % RDI: 4% calcium, 21% iron, 9% vit A, 23% vit C, 14% folate.

BEEF BROCHETTES

450 g	beef sirloin grilling steak (1 inch thick)
2 tbsp	adobo sauce
2 tsp	chopped garlic
¼ tsp	each salt and pepper
1	red onion

MELON CUCUMBER RELISH

1 cup	diced peeled honeydew melon
½ cup	diced seeded English cucumber
¼ cup	chopped fresh parsley
2 tbsp	white wine vinegar
2 tbsp	olive oil
1 tsp	granulated sugar
¼ tsp	each salt and pepper

TIP FROM THE TEST KITCHEN

Canned chipotle peppers come packed in adobo, a spicy, smoky, tomato-based sauce. You can freeze any leftover chipotles and sauce for future use.

Pork Souvlaki
WITH TZATZIKI

HANDS-ON TIME	TOTAL TIME	MAKES
15 MINUTES	30 MINUTES	4 SERVINGS

TZATZIKI

1 cup	shredded seeded cucumber
½ tsp	salt
¾ cup	Balkan-style plain yogurt
2	cloves garlic, minced
2 tbsp	chopped fresh dill (optional)
1 tbsp	lemon juice

SOUVLAKI

675 g	pork tenderloin
2 tbsp	lemon juice
1 tbsp	olive oil
1	large clove garlic, minced
½ tsp	dried oregano
½ tsp	salt
¼ tsp	pepper
4	Greek-style pocketless pitas
2	plum tomatoes, sliced
half	red onion, sliced
1 cup	shredded romaine lettuce

TZATZIKI In bowl, mix cucumber with salt; let stand for 10 minutes. Squeeze out excess liquid. Combine cucumber, yogurt, garlic, dill (if using) and lemon juice.

SOUVLAKI Meanwhile, trim pork and cut into 1-inch cubes. In large bowl, whisk together lemon juice, oil, garlic, oregano, salt and pepper; add pork and stir to coat. Cover and marinate for 10 minutes. *(Make-ahead: Refrigerate for up to 6 hours.)*

Thread pork onto metal skewers; brush with remaining marinade. Place on greased grill over medium-high heat; close lid and grill, turning halfway through, until juices run clear when pork is pierced and just a hint of pink remains inside, about 12 minutes. Remove from skewers. Serve on pitas with tomatoes, red onion, lettuce and tzatziki.

NUTRITIONAL INFORMATION, PER SERVING: about 463 cal, 46 g pro, 10 g total fat (4 g sat. fat), 44 g carb (3 g dietary fibre), 100 mg chol, 863 mg sodium, 910 mg potassium. % RDI: 14% calcium, 28% iron, 12% vit A, 22% vit C, 49% folate.

TIP FROM THE TEST KITCHEN
Don't forget to squeeze liquid out of the salted cucumber to keep your tzatziki thick and creamy.

Sesame Chicken & Radish Skewers
WITH ORANGE SALAD

HANDS-ON TIME	TOTAL TIME	MAKES
30 MINUTES	30 MINUTES	4 SERVINGS

p.159

CHICKEN AND RADISH SKEWERS Whisk together honey, soy sauce, sesame oil and garlic; set aside.

Sprinkle chicken with ½ tsp of the salt and the pepper. Thread 3 pieces onto each of eight 6-inch metal or soaked wooden skewers. Place on greased grill over medium-high heat; close lid and grill, turning once, until no longer pink inside, about 8 minutes. Brush with some of the honey mixture; grill, turning and brushing with some of the remaining honey mixture halfway through, for 1 minute. Transfer skewers to plate; sprinkle with two-thirds of the sesame seeds.

While chicken is grilling, thread 3 radishes onto each of four 6-inch metal or soaked wooden skewers. Place on greased grill over medium-high heat; close lid and grill, turning once, until tender and slightly charred, about 6 minutes. Brush with some of the remaining honey mixture; grill, turning and brushing with some of the remaining honey mixture halfway through, for 1 minute.

Remove radishes from skewers and place in bowl; drizzle with any remaining honey mixture. Sprinkle with remaining sesame seeds and salt.

ORANGE SALAD Meanwhile, segment orange, squeezing 1 tsp juice from remaining membranes into large bowl; set segments aside.

Whisk oil, vinegar, honey, wasabi, salt and pepper into orange juice. *(Make-ahead: Refrigerate in airtight container for up to 24 hours.)* Add lettuce, avocado and reserved orange segments; gently toss to coat. Serve with chicken and radishes.

CHICKEN AND RADISH SKEWERS

2 tbsp	liquid honey
1 tbsp	sodium-reduced soy sauce
1 tsp	sesame oil
1	clove garlic, finely grated or pressed
450 g	boneless skinless chicken breasts, cut in 24 cubes
¾ tsp	salt
¼ tsp	pepper
1 tbsp	sesame seeds, toasted
12	small radishes, trimmed

ORANGE SALAD

1	orange
4 tsp	extra-virgin olive oil
1 tsp	seasoned rice vinegar
½ tsp	liquid honey
½ tsp	prepared wasabi
pinch	each salt and pepper
4 cups	chopped green leaf lettuce
1	avocado, peeled, pitted and sliced

NUTRITIONAL INFORMATION, PER SERVING: about 326 cal, 28 g pro, 16 g total fat (3 g sat. fat), 19 g carb (5 g dietary fibre, 12 g sugar), 66 mg chol, 663 mg sodium, 755 mg potassium. % RDI: 4% calcium, 10% iron, 17% vit A, 35% vit C, 34% folate.

Teriyaki Chicken Skewers

HANDS-ON TIME	TOTAL TIME	MAKES
35 MINUTES	35 MINUTES	6 SERVINGS

TERIYAKI SAUCE

⅓ **cup**	sodium-reduced soy sauce
3 tbsp	mirin
1 tbsp	packed brown sugar
1 tsp	minced peeled fresh ginger
1	clove garlic, minced

CHICKEN SKEWERS

450 g	boneless skinless chicken thighs, cut in 1-inch chunks
4	green onions (white and light green parts only), cut crosswise in 1-inch pieces
1 tbsp	vegetable oil
¼ tsp	each salt and pepper

TERIYAKI SAUCE In saucepan, bring soy sauce, mirin, brown sugar, ginger, garlic and ¼ cup water to boil. Reduce heat and simmer until reduced to about ⅓ cup, 7 to 9 minutes. Strain through fine-mesh sieve; discard solids. *(Make-ahead: Refrigerate in airtight container for up to 5 days.)*

CHICKEN SKEWERS While sauce is simmering, alternately thread chicken and green onions onto 6 soaked wooden skewers. *(Make-ahead: Refrigerate in airtight container for up to 24 hours.)* Brush all over with oil; sprinkle with salt and pepper.

Place on greased grill over medium-high heat; close lid and grill, turning occasionally and brushing with 2 tbsp of the teriyaki sauce during final minute of cooking. Grill until chicken is no longer pink inside, about 12 minutes. Transfer to serving platter; brush with remaining teriyaki sauce.

(A)

NUTRITIONAL INFORMATION, PER SERVING: about 141 cal, 15 g pro, 6 g total fat (1 g sat. fat), 5 g carb (trace dietary fibre, 3 g sugar), 55 mg chol, 442 mg sodium, 182 mg potassium. % RDI: 2% calcium, 8% iron, 2% vit A, 2% vit C, 5% folate.

TIP FROM THE TEST KITCHEN
Make a double batch of the teriyaki sauce to use in stir-fries and noodle dishes or to glaze grilled tofu.

Japanese-Style Stuffed Peppers

HANDS-ON TIME	TOTAL TIME	MAKES
30 MINUTES	30 MINUTES	6 SERVINGS

In bowl, whisk together 1 tbsp of the mirin and the miso paste until smooth. Stir in chicken, green onions, mushrooms, ginger, garlic, salt and pepper until combined. Spoon into jalapeño peppers. Thread 2 of the jalapeño pepper halves crosswise onto 2 soaked wooden skewers. Repeat with remaining jalapeño pepper halves and 10 additional skewers. *(Make-ahead: Refrigerate in airtight container for up to 24 hours.)*

Place, cut side down, on greased grill over medium heat; close lid and grill for 5 minutes. Turn skewers; grill until chicken is no longer pink inside and instant-read thermometer inserted in centres reads 165°F, about 10 minutes.

Whisk together remaining mirin, the soy sauce and oil; brush over chicken before serving.

2 tbsp	mirin
1 tbsp	white miso paste
225 g	ground chicken
⅓ cup	minced green onions (about 3)
⅓ cup	finely chopped shiitake mushrooms
1 tsp	minced peeled fresh ginger
1	clove garlic, minced
¼ tsp	each salt and pepper
6	large jalapeño peppers, halved lengthwise and seeded
1 tsp	sodium-reduced soy sauce
½ tsp	vegetable oil

NUTRITIONAL INFORMATION, PER SERVING: about 128 cal, 9 g pro, 6 g total fat (1 g sat. fat), 10 g carb (3 g dietary fibre, 5 g sugar), 29 mg chol, 277 mg sodium, 274 mg potassium. % RDI: 2% calcium, 9% iron, 5% vit A, 37% vit C, 12% folate.

TIP FROM THE TEST KITCHEN

To temper the spiciness of jalapeños in this and other dishes, remove the seeds and white membranes; leave them in for extra heat.

Threading the skewers through both the peppers and the chicken will help keep the filling in place as it cooks.

Lamb Koftas
WITH CUCUMBER RAITA

HANDS-ON TIME 30 MINUTES	TOTAL TIME 30 MINUTES	MAKES 4 SERVINGS

CUCUMBER RAITA

½ cup	plain Balkan-style yogurt
⅓ cup	grated peeled cucumber, squeezed and patted dry
2 tbsp	finely chopped fresh mint
2 tsp	lime juice
1	small clove garlic, finely grated or pressed
pinch	each salt and pepper

KOFTAS

450 g	ground lamb
half	small onion, finely chopped
⅓ cup	chopped fresh cilantro
4	cloves garlic, minced
2 tsp	chili powder
1 tsp	ground coriander
½ tsp	ground cumin
¼ tsp	each paprika, salt and pepper
2 tsp	olive oil
8	small (6-inch) pitas
1 cup	coleslaw mix or shredded cabbage
1	lime, cut in wedges (optional)

CUCUMBER RAITA Stir together yogurt, cucumber, mint, lime juice, garlic, salt and pepper; set aside.

KOFTAS In large bowl, stir together lamb, onion, cilantro, garlic, chili powder, coriander, cumin, paprika, salt and pepper. Form into eight 4-inch long sausage-shaped ovals, pressing to pack.

Thread onto 8 metal or soaked wooden skewers; brush koftas all over with oil. Place on greased grill over medium-high heat; close lid and grill, turning once, until no longer pink inside and instant-read thermometer inserted in several reads 160°F, 8 to 10 minutes.

While koftas are cooking, grill pitas over medium-high heat, turning once, until warmed and grill-marked, about 2 minutes. Top pitas with cucumber raita, coleslaw mix and koftas. Serve with lime wedges (if using).

NUTRITIONAL INFORMATION, PER SERVING: about 571 cal, 34 g pro, 16 g total fat (6 g sat. fat), 74 g carb (4 g dietary fibre, 4 g sugar), 60 mg chol, 988 mg sodium, 604 mg potassium. % RDI: 18% calcium, 40% iron, 11% vit A, 15% vit C, 55% folate.

TIP FROM THE TEST KITCHEN
These koftas are also delicious with hummus and a simple cucumber and tomato salad.

Grilled Sesame Edamame

HANDS-ON TIME	TOTAL TIME	MAKES
15 MINUTES	15 MINUTES	12 SERVINGS

Thread edamame onto metal or soaked wooden skewers; brush with sesame oil. Place on grill over medium-high heat; close lid and grill, turning once, until tender and slightly charred, 6 to 8 minutes. Remove from skewers; toss with sesame seeds and salt. Serve warm.

500 g	frozen whole edamame (in shell), thawed
2 tsp	sesame oil
1½ tsp	sesame seeds
½ tsp	sea salt

NUTRITIONAL INFORMATION, PER SERVING: about 33 cal, 3 g pro, 2 g total fat (trace sat. fat), 2 g carb (2 g dietary fibre, 1 g sugar), 0 mg chol, 66 mg sodium, 135 mg potassium. % RDI: 2% calcium, 4% iron, 3% vit C, 30% folate.

Mushroom Skewers

HANDS-ON TIME	TOTAL TIME	MAKES
15 MINUTES	15 MINUTES	6 SERVINGS

In large bowl, stir together butter, oil, parsley, garlic, salt and pepper. Add mushrooms and toss to coat. Reserving any remaining butter mixture, thread mushrooms onto metal or soaked wooden skewers.

Place on greased grill over medium-high heat; leave lid open and grill, turning occasionally and brushing with reserved butter mixture, until mushrooms are tender, about 5 minutes.

2 tbsp	butter, melted
1 tbsp	olive oil
1 tbsp	chopped fresh parsley
2	cloves garlic, minced
pinch	salt
pinch	pepper
2	pkg (each 227 g) cremini mushrooms

NUTRITIONAL INFORMATION, PER SERVING: about 71 cal, 2 g pro, 6 g total fat (3 g sat. fat), 3 g carb (2 g dietary fibre, 1 g sugar), 10 mg chol, 32 mg sodium, 317 mg potassium. % RDI: 1% calcium, 2% iron, 4% vit A, 2% vit C, 4% folate.

p.44

Herbed Mini Potato Skewers

HANDS-ON TIME	TOTAL TIME	MAKES
30 MINUTES	40 MINUTES	10 TO 12 SERVINGS

30	mini yellow-fleshed potatoes or mini white potatoes, scrubbed (about 675 g total)
30	mini red potatoes, scrubbed (about 675 g total)
⅔ cup	butter, melted
2	cloves garlic, pressed or grated
1 tbsp	finely chopped fresh parsley
2 tsp	finely chopped fresh rosemary
¼ tsp	each salt and pepper

In large saucepan of boiling salted water, cook yellow-fleshed and red potatoes until tender, about 15 minutes. Drain and let cool slightly. *(Make-ahead: Cover and refrigerate for up to 24 hours.)*

Stir together butter, garlic, parsley, rosemary, salt and pepper. Alternating colours, thread potatoes onto metal skewers. Brush with some of the butter mixture.

Place skewers on greased grill over medium-high heat; close lid and grill, turning and brushing frequently with butter mixture, until potatoes are hot and golden, about 8 minutes.

NUTRITIONAL INFORMATION, PER EACH OF 12 SERVINGS: about 142 cal, 2 g pro, 7 g total fat (4 g sat. fat), 19 g carb (2 g dietary fibre, 1 g sugar), 18 mg chol, 310 mg sodium, 417 mg potassium. % RDI: 1% calcium, 6% iron, 6% vit A, 23% vit C, 6% folate.

Ⓥ

8+

TIP FROM THE TEST KITCHEN
If you have leftovers, cut the potatoes in half and add to a breakfast frittata or reheat in a lightly oiled skillet over medium heat.

Jerk Tofu Skewers
WITH GRILLED COLESLAW

HANDS-ON TIME 15 MINUTES	TOTAL TIME 35 MINUTES	MAKES 4 TO 6 SERVINGS

GRILLED COLESLAW Cut cabbage into six wedges; core. Cut red onion into 3 wedges. Place on greased grill over medium heat until outer layers start to soften, about 10 minutes. Let cool slightly; slice thinly.

In large bowl, toss sliced cabbage, red onion, carrot, mayonnaise, vinegar, salt, pepper and celery seed.

JERK BARBECUE SAUCE In saucepan, bring tomatoes, molasses, jerk sauce, vinegar and thyme to boil. Reduce heat and simmer until reduced to ½ cup, 10 to 15 minutes.

TOFU SKEWERS Meanwhile, cut tofu into 24 cubes. In bowl, gently toss tofu, garlic, soy sauce and oil; let stand for 10 minutes.

Cut each sweet pepper into 24 pieces; cut each green onion in half. Thread vegetables and tofu alternately onto soaked wooden skewers; brush with jerk barbecue sauce.

Place on greased grill over medium-high heat; close lid and grill, turning and brushing with sauce, until vegetables are tender and slightly browned. Serve with grilled coleslaw.

NUTRITIONAL INFORMATION, PER EACH OF 6 SERVINGS: about 201 cal, 9 g pro, 10 g total fat (2 g sat. fat), 23 g carb (4 g dietary fibre), 2 mg chol, 639 mg sodium, 575 mg potassium. % RDI: 22% calcium, 24% iron, 31% vit A, 197% vit C, 28% folate.

TIP FROM THE TEST KITCHEN
Be sure to buy firm or extra-firm tofu for grilling; soft or silken tofu is too delicate and will fall apart on the grill.

GRILLED COLESLAW
1	small cabbage
half	red onion
1	carrot, grated
2 tbsp	mayonnaise
2 tbsp	malt vinegar or cider vinegar
¼ tsp	each salt, pepper and celery seed

JERK BARBECUE SAUCE
1 cup	bottled strained tomatoes (passata)
2 tbsp	fancy molasses
1 tbsp	prepared jerk sauce
2 tsp	malt vinegar
¼ tsp	dried thyme

TOFU SKEWERS
1	pkg (454 g) firm or extra-firm tofu
2	cloves garlic, finely minced
2 tbsp	sodium-reduced soy sauce
1 tbsp	vegetable oil
1	each sweet red, orange and yellow pepper
6	green onions (white parts only)

Asian-Style Salmon Kabobs
WITH BABY BOK CHOY

HANDS-ON TIME	TOTAL TIME	MAKES
10 MINUTES	30 MINUTES	4 SERVINGS

SALMON KABOBS

4 tsp	soy sauce
1 tbsp	oyster sauce
2 tsp	lemon juice
2 tsp	sesame oil
1 tsp	liquid honey
¼ tsp	hot pepper flakes
4	skinless salmon fillets (each about 170 g), cut crosswise in 4 pieces

BABY BOK CHOY

1 tbsp	butter
1	shallot, minced
2 tsp	minced fresh ginger
1	clove garlic, minced
4	baby bok choy, halved lengthwise
¼ tsp	salt
1 tsp	sesame oil

SALMON KABOBS In baking dish, combine soy sauce, oyster sauce, lemon juice, sesame oil, honey and hot pepper flakes. Add fish, turning to coat; let stand for 10 minutes.

Thread fish onto metal or soaked wooden skewers. Place on greased grill over medium-high heat; close lid and grill until fish is opaque, 8 to 10 minutes.

BABY BOK CHOY Meanwhile, in skillet, melt butter over medium-high heat; sauté shallot, ginger and garlic for 1 minute. Add ¼ cup water, the bok choy and salt; cover and steam for 2 minutes. Uncover and cook until tender-crisp, 2 to 3 minutes. Drizzle with sesame oil. Serve with salmon kabobs.

NUTRITIONAL INFORMATION, PER SERVING: about 338 cal, 31 g pro, 22 g total fat (6 g sat. fat), 4 g carb (1 g dietary fibre), 91 mg chol, 483 mg sodium, 835 mg potassium. % RDI: 9% calcium, 10% iron, 39% vit A, 43% vit C, 36% folate.

(30)

TIP FROM THE TEST KITCHEN
Don't marinate fish for longer than about 30 minutes, especially if the marinade is acidic—the fish's texture will become mushy.

SAUCES

Maple Mustard Basting Sauce

HANDS-ON TIME 10 MINUTES
TOTAL TIME 10 MINUTES
MAKES ABOUT 2 CUPS

2 tbsp	vegetable oil
2	small onions, chopped
4	cloves garlic, minced
⅔ cup	dry white wine
½ cup	maple syrup
¼ cup	cider vinegar
2 tsp	dry mustard
½ tsp	each salt and pepper
⅓ cup	Dijon mustard
3 tbsp	unsalted butter

In saucepan, heat oil over medium heat; cook onions and garlic, stirring often, until fragrant and golden, about 2 minutes.

Stir in wine and bring to boil; boil for 1 minute. Add maple syrup, vinegar, dry mustard, salt and pepper; return to boil and boil until slightly syrupy, about 3 minutes.

Stir in Dijon mustard and butter until melted. Let cool slightly. Transfer to blender and blend until smooth. *(Make-ahead: Refrigerate in airtight container for up to 2 weeks.)*

NUTRITIONAL INFORMATION, PER ¼ CUP: about 153 cal, 1 g pro, 9 g total fat (3 g sat. fat), 17 g carb (1 g dietary fibre, 12 g sugar), 11 mg chol, 282 mg sodium, 115 mg potassium. % RDI: 4% calcium, 5% iron, 4% vit A, 2% vit C, 2% folate.

Honey Ginger Basting Sauce

HANDS-ON TIME 15 MINUTES
TOTAL TIME 15 MINUTES
MAKES ABOUT 2 CUPS

2 tbsp	vegetable oil
6	shallots, minced
6	cloves garlic, minced
6 tbsp	grated fresh ginger
½ cup	hoisin sauce
½ cup	liquid honey
2 tbsp	rice vinegar
2 tsp	sesame oil
½ tsp	hot pepper flakes
2 tsp	cornstarch

In saucepan, heat oil over medium heat; cook shallots, garlic and ginger, stirring occasionally, until fragrant and golden, about 2 minutes.

Stir in hoisin sauce, honey, ¼ cup water, the vinegar, sesame oil and hot pepper flakes; bring to boil. Boil until thickened slightly, 2 to 3 minutes.

Whisk cornstarch with ¼ cup water; whisk into sauce and simmer until thickened, about 1 minute. *(Make-ahead: Refrigerate in airtight container for up to 2 weeks.)*

NUTRITIONAL INFORMATION, PER ¼ CUP: about 159 cal, 1 g pro, 5 g total fat (1 g sat. fat), 29 g carb (1 g dietary fibre, 22 g sugar), 0 mg chol, 262 mg sodium, 103 mg potassium. % RDI: 1% calcium, 3% iron, 1% vit A, 2% vit C, 3% folate.

Sweet-and-Sour Barbecue Sauce

HANDS-ON TIME 15 MINUTES
TOTAL TIME 15 MINUTES
MAKES ABOUT 1¾ CUPS

2 tsp	vegetable oil
1	onion, finely diced
2	cloves garlic, minced
⅔ cup	bottled strained tomatoes (passata)
1	canned chipotle pepper in adobo sauce, chopped
2 tbsp	tomato paste
1 tbsp	red wine vinegar
2 tsp	packed brown sugar
pinch	salt

In saucepan, heat oil over medium heat; cook onion and garlic, stirring occasionally, until tender and light golden, about 5 minutes.

Stir in strained tomatoes, chipotle pepper, tomato paste, vinegar, brown sugar and salt; bring to boil. Reduce heat and simmer until thickened, 10 to 12 minutes. Let cool slightly. Using immersion blender, purée until smooth.

NUTRITIONAL INFORMATION, PER 1 TBSP: about 21 cal, trace pro, 1 g total fat (trace sat. fat), 3 g carb (trace dietary fibre, 2 g sugar), 0 mg chol, 41 mg sodium, 71 mg potassium. % RDI: 1% calcium, 3% iron, 1% vit A, 2% vit C, 1% folate.

Grilled Asparagus Pizza

HANDS-ON TIME	TOTAL TIME	MAKES
30 MINUTES	30 MINUTES	4 SERVINGS

2 tbsp	olive oil
2	cloves garlic, finely grated or pressed
2 tsp	dried oregano
½ tsp	grated lemon zest
¼ tsp	hot pepper flakes
pinch	each salt and pepper
1	bunch asparagus (about 450 g), trimmed
350 g	prepared pizza dough
1⅓ cups	shredded mozzarella cheese
½ cup	halved cherry tomatoes

Whisk together half of the oil, the garlic, oregano, lemon zest, hot pepper flakes, salt and pepper; set aside.

Toss asparagus with 1 tsp of the remaining oil. Place on greased grill over medium-high heat; close lid and grill, turning often, until grill-marked and tender-crisp, 6 to 8 minutes. Set aside.

On lightly floured work surface, roll or press out dough to form 16- × 8½-inch oval. Brush 1 side with 1 tsp of the remaining oil. Place, oiled side down, on greased grill over medium heat; leave lid open and grill until bubbles form on top and bottom is grill-marked, about 3 minutes. Brush with remaining oil.

Reduce heat to medium-low; flip crust and brush with garlic mixture. Top with mozzarella, asparagus and tomatoes. Close lid and grill until mozzarella is melted and bottom of crust is browned, 5 to 8 minutes.

NUTRITIONAL INFORMATION, PER SERVING: about 436 cal, 17 g pro, 22 g total fat (8 g sat. fat), 45 g carb (4 g dietary fibre, 6 g sugar), 34 mg chol, 572 mg sodium, 364 mg potassium. % RDI: 31% calcium, 26% iron, 17% vit A, 15% vit C, 86% folate.

TIP FROM THE TEST KITCHEN

The pizza dough will be easier to handle if you take it out of the fridge about 15 minutes before using it. Because barbecue temperatures vary, check the bottom of the crust often while grilling to avoid burning it.

Gouda & Smoked Tomato Bruschetta

HANDS-ON TIME	TOTAL TIME	MAKES
30 MINUTES	4½ HOURS	6 PIECES

Soak 3 cups wood chips for 1 hour; drain. For gas barbecue, heat 1 burner of 2-burner barbecue or outer 2 burners of 3-burner barbecue to medium heat. Wrap soaked chips in heavy-duty foil to make packet; poke several holes in top. Remove one rack and place packet directly over lit burner; close lid. (For charcoal barbecue, push coals to one side; sprinkle soaked chips directly on coals.)

In bowl, gently toss tomatoes with 2 tsp of the oil. Arrange tomatoes, cut sides up, on rimmed baking sheet. Place baking sheet on rack over unlit burner; close lid and cook on low heat (about 275°F) until tomatoes are shrivelled and appear dry yet still plump, about 3 hours.

Remove tomatoes from grill; set aside. Remove wood chips and return rack over lit burner. Leaving 1 burner unlit, heat remaining burner(s) to medium-high.

Brush both sides of bread slices with remaining oil. Place on greased grill over lit burner; close lid and grill, turning occasionally, until crisp and grill-marked, about 4 minutes. Sprinkle slices with Gouda and move over unlit burner; close lid and cook until cheese is melted, 4 to 6 minutes. Top with tomatoes; sprinkle with salt, pepper and basil.

18	cocktail tomatoes, halved crosswise
2 tbsp	olive oil
6	slices (¾-inch thick) crusty Italian bread or French bread
1½ cups	shredded Gouda cheese
pinch	each salt and pepper
¼ cup	torn fresh basil leaves

NUTRITIONAL INFORMATION, PER PIECE: about 267 cal, 12 g pro, 14 g total fat (6 g sat. fat), 25 g carb (3 g dietary fibre, 6 g sugar), 33 mg chol, 442 mg sodium, 506 mg potassium. % RDI: 23% calcium, 12% iron, 21% vit A, 37% vit C, 33% folate.

TIP FROM THE TEST KITCHEN

To infuse the tomatoes with deep smoky flavour, use strongly flavoured wood chips, such as hickory.

Bacon & Feta Mini Pizzas

HANDS-ON TIME 20 MINUTES	TOTAL TIME 20 MINUTES	MAKES 12 MINI PIZZAS

4	strips bacon
12	mini pita breads
4 tsp	red pepper jelly
¼ cup	thinly sliced red onion
¼ cup	crumbled feta cheese

In skillet, cook bacon over medium heat, turning once, until crisp, about 8 minutes. Transfer to paper towel–lined plate to drain. Chop bacon; set aside. *(Make-ahead: Refrigerate in airtight container for up to 24 hours.)*

Place pitas on rimmed baking sheet. Spread jelly over tops; sprinkle with bacon, red onion and feta.

Using metal spatula, carefully transfer pitas to greased grill over medium heat; close lid and grill until warm, about 4 minutes.

p.75

NUTRITIONAL INFORMATION, PER MINI PIZZA: about 60 cal, 2 g pro, 2 g total fat (1 g sat. fat), 8 g carb (trace dietary fibre, 1 g sugar), 5 mg chol, 152 mg sodium, 34 mg potassium. % RDI: 2% calcium, 3% iron, 4% folate.

TIP FROM THE TEST KITCHEN
Grilled tostadas, pizzas and similar flatbreads aren't on the grill long enough to cook raw ingredients. Top them with precooked vegetables (or ones that don't need cooking), and only use cooked or ready-to-eat meats.

Grilled Panzanella Bites

HANDS-ON TIME	TOTAL TIME	MAKES
25 MINUTES	2½ HOURS	10 TO 12 SERVINGS

In bowl, whisk together ¼ cup of the oil, the vinegar, garlic, salt and pepper. Add bocconcini and red onion; cover and refrigerate for 2 hours. *(Make-ahead: Refrigerate for up to 24 hours.)*

Brush baguette slices with remaining oil. Place on greased grill over medium heat; grill, turning occasionally, until crisp and golden, about 5 minutes.

Meanwhile, add tomatoes and basil to bocconcini mixture; toss to combine. Serve on toasted baguette slices.

NUTRITIONAL INFORMATION, PER EACH OF 12 SERVINGS: about 187 cal, 6 g pro, 10 g total fat (3 g sat. fat), 18 g carb (2 g dietary fibre, 2 g sugar), 11 mg chol, 276 mg sodium, 149 mg potassium. % RDI: 10% calcium, 7% iron, 6% vit A, 10% vit C, 14% folate.

⅓ cup	olive oil
¼ cup	red wine vinegar or white wine vinegar
2	cloves garlic, minced
½ tsp	salt
¼ tsp	pepper
1 cup	mini pearl bocconcini
½ cup	finely chopped red onion
1	large baguette, diagonally sliced ½-inch thick
4 cups	halved grape tomatoes
½ cup	chopped fresh basil

VARIATION
Village Salad Bites
Omit salt. Replace bocconcini with ¾ cup crumbled feta cheese. Replace basil with mint. Add ⅓ cup chopped Kalamata olives with tomatoes.

Black Bean Tostadas
WITH MANGO AVOCADO SALAD

HANDS-ON TIME	TOTAL TIME	MAKES
15 MINUTES	15 MINUTES	4 SERVINGS

TOSTADAS

1	can (540 mL) black beans, drained and rinsed
3 tbsp	light sour cream
1½ tsp	chili powder
4	soft flour tortillas (6 inches)
1 cup	shredded Monterey Jack cheese

MANGO AVOCADO SALAD

3 tbsp	olive oil
1 tbsp	lime juice
1 tsp	liquid honey
¼ tsp	chili powder
pinch	each salt and pepper
1	mango, peeled, pitted and cut in 1-inch chunks
1	avocado, peeled, pitted and cut in 1-inch chunks
3½ cups	packed watercress (about 1 bunch)
⅓ cup	thinly sliced red onion

TOSTADAS In bowl using potato masher, roughly mash beans. Stir in sour cream and chili powder.

Spread one-quarter of the bean mixture onto each tortilla, leaving ½-inch border. Sprinkle with Monterey Jack. Place on greased grill over medium-low heat; close lid and grill until cheese is melted and tortillas are crisp, 6 to 7 minutes.

MANGO AVOCADO SALAD While tostadas are grilling, in large bowl, whisk together oil, lime juice, honey, chili powder, salt and pepper. Add mango, avocado, watercress and red onion; toss to coat. Serve over tostadas.

NUTRITIONAL INFORMATION, PER SERVING: about 523 cal, 18 g pro, 30 g total fat (9 g sat. fat), 50 g carb (13 g dietary fibre, 11 g sugar), 29 mg chol, 742 mg sodium, 841 mg potassium. % RDI: 28% calcium, 24% iron, 24% vit A, 60% vit C, 67% folate.

TIP FROM THE TEST KITCHEN

To choose a ripe mango, squeeze it gently; it should yield slightly. Some (but not all) mango varieties produce a fruity aroma at the stem end when ripe.

Grilled Radishes
WITH CREAMY CILANTRO DIP

HANDS-ON TIME	TOTAL TIME	MAKES
15 MINUTES	15 MINUTES	10 SERVINGS

(30)

(V)

(8+)

CREAMY CILANTRO DIP Whisk together mayonnaise, sour cream, cilantro, mint, lime juice and pepper; set aside. *(Make-ahead: Cover and refrigerate for up to 24 hours.)*

RADISHES In bowl, toss together radishes, butter, lime juice, honey and pepper. Place on lightly greased grill over medium-high heat; close lid and grill, turning once, until tender and slightly charred, about 5 minutes. Return to bowl; toss with salt. Serve warm with dip.

NUTRITIONAL INFORMATION, PER SERVING: about 69 cal, 1 g pro, 6 g total fat (2 g sat. fat), 3 g carb (1 g dietary fibre, 2 g sugar), 7 mg chol, 117 mg sodium, 111 mg potassium. % RDI: 2% calcium, 1% iron, 3% vit A, 8% vit C, 4% folate.

CREAMY CILANTRO DIP

¼ **cup**	mayonnaise
¼ **cup**	sour cream
2 **tbsp**	chopped fresh cilantro
1 **tbsp**	finely chopped fresh mint
½ **tsp**	lime juice
pinch	pepper

RADISHES

20	large radishes, halved lengthwise
1 **tbsp**	butter, melted
2 **tsp**	lime juice
1 **tsp**	liquid honey
pinch	pepper
¼ **tsp**	salt

TIP FROM THE TEST KITCHEN
Grilling radishes softens their peppery bite, which is caused by natural chemicals similar to those in mustard and wasabi. Skewer small radishes or use a grill basket to keep them from falling through the grates.

Charred Artichokes
WITH LEMON, CAPERS & PARMESAN

HANDS-ON TIME	TOTAL TIME	MAKES
10 MINUTES	25 MINUTES	4 SERVINGS

1	lemon
4	large artichokes, trimmed and halved
2 tbsp	olive oil
¼ tsp	salt
½ cup	shaved Parmesan cheese
2 tbsp	finely chopped basil
1 tbsp	capers, drained and rinsed
pinch	hot pepper flakes
4	lemon wedges

Halve and juice lemon. Reserving 1 tbsp lemon juice, add lemon halves, juice and artichokes to large saucepan of boiling salted water. Bring to boil; cook until artichokes are fork-tender, about 10 minutes. Discard lemon halves; drain artichokes and chill in ice water; drain well. Remove and discard chokes.

In bowl, toss together artichokes, 1 tbsp of the oil and the salt. Place on greased grill over medium-high heat; grill, turning occasionally, until grill-marked and heated through, about 4 minutes. Transfer to serving platter. Sprinkle with Parmesan, basil, capers, and hot pepper flakes. Drizzle with remaining oil and reserved lemon juice. Serve with lemon wedges.

NUTRITIONAL INFORMATION, PER SERVING: about 146 cal, 6 g pro, 9 g total fat (2 g sat. fat), 14 g carb (10 g dietary fibre, 1 g sugar), 4 mg chol, 659 mg sodium, 362 mg potassium. % RDI: 9% calcium, 6% iron, 2% vit A, 18% vit C, 50% folate.

TIP FROM THE TEST KITCHEN
To prep artichokes, trim the top third of the bud and remove the thick outer leaves. Use a vegetable peeler to strip the outer layer of the base and stem. Halve the artichoke lengthwise. To prevent browning, rub cut surfaces with lemon juice and place trimmed artichokes in a bowl of ice water with a squeeze of lemon juice.

Balsamic Vegetables

HANDS-ON TIME	TOTAL TIME	MAKES
25 MINUTES	2½ HOURS	10 TO 12 SERVINGS

In bowl, combine vinegar, garlic, honey, salt and pepper; slowly whisk in oil until combined.

Cut each zucchini in half crosswise; cut lengthwise into ½-inch thick slices. Place in large dish. Cut red onion into ½-inch thick rounds; add to dish.

Core and seed sweet peppers; cut into large chunks and add to dish. Remove stems and gills from mushrooms; cut caps into quarters and add to dish. Pour marinade over vegetables; cover and let stand at room temperature for 2 hours, tossing occasionally.

Place vegetables on greased grill over medium-high heat; close lid and grill, basting frequently with marinade, until tender, about 12 minutes. Serve sprinkled with parsley.

⅓ cup	balsamic vinegar
3	cloves garlic, pressed or grated
2 tsp	liquid honey
¼ tsp	each salt and pepper
½ cup	olive oil
3	large green and/or yellow zucchini (about 675 g total)
1	large red onion
2	sweet red, orange and/or yellow peppers
4	portobello mushrooms
¼ cup	chopped fresh flat-leaf parsley

NUTRITIONAL INFORMATION, PER EACH OF 12 SERVINGS: about 97 cal, 2 g pro, 7 g total fat (1 g sat. fat), 9 g carb (2 g dietary fibre, 4 g sugar), 0 mg chol, 41 mg sodium, 309 mg potassium. % RDI: 2% calcium, 4% iron, 10% vit A, 60% vit C, 10% folate.

TIP FROM THE TEST KITCHEN

When you're grilling vegetables, make extra for easy vegetarian sandwiches the next day. Spread chèvre, herbed cream cheese or other soft cheese on crusty rolls or baguettes, and sandwich with the vegetables.

Cilantro-Jalapeño Grilled Tofu Salad

HANDS-ON TIME	TOTAL TIME	MAKES
20 MINUTES	20 MINUTES	4 SERVINGS

1	pkg (about 450 g) firm tofu, drained
½ tsp	salt
¼ cup	lime juice
4 tsp	liquid honey
half	jalapeño, seeded and minced
2	cloves garlic, minced
½ tsp	each chili powder and pepper
¼ cup	chopped fresh cilantro
2	green onions, minced
¼ cup	extra-virgin olive oil
6 cups	lightly packed mixed baby greens
1 cup	cherry tomatoes, halved
1	small carrot, shredded

Cut tofu into 12 scant ½-inch thick slices. Sprinkle tofu with a pinch of the salt; set aside.

In large bowl, whisk together lime juice, honey, jalapeño, garlic, chili powder, pepper and remaining salt. Stir in cilantro, green onions and oil.

Brush tofu all over with ¼ cup of the dressing. Place on greased grill over medium-high heat; close lid and grill, turning once, until golden and heated through, 6 to 8 minutes. Brush on another ¼ cup of the dressing.

Toss together baby greens, cherry tomatoes, carrot and remaining dressing. Serve with tofu.

NUTRITIONAL INFORMATION, PER SERVING: about 323 cal, 18 g pro, 22 g total fat (3 g sat. fat), 17 g carb (3 g dietary fibre, 9 g sugar), 0 mg chol, 356 mg sodium, 658 mg potassium. % RDI: 24% calcium, 25% iron, 102% vit A, 37% vit C, 58% folate.

TIP FROM THE TEST KITCHEN
If the tofu slices are very moist, squeeze them gently to help extract some liquid before you brush the slices with dressing.

GRILLED GARAM MASALA CORN
(OPPOSITE, TOP)

Grilled Garam Masala Corn

HANDS-ON TIME	TOTAL TIME	MAKES
20 MINUTES	20 MINUTES	10 SERVINGS

In small bowl, stir together butter, green onions, garlic, garam masala, pepper, cinnamon and salt. *(Make-ahead: Cover and refrigerate for up to 5 days. Let soften at room temperature for 15 minutes.)*

Place corn cobs on greased grill over medium-high heat; close lid and grill, turning occasionally, for 8 minutes. Continue grilling, brushing occasionally with butter mixture, until grill-marked and tender, 12 to 15 minutes.

⅔ cup	butter, softened
2	green onions, minced
2	cloves garlic, minced
2 tsp	garam masala
½ tsp	pepper
pinch	each cinnamon and salt
10	corn cobs, husked

NUTRITIONAL INFORMATION, PER SERVING: about 242 cal, 4 g pro, 14 g total fat (8 g sat. fat), 31 g carb (4 g dietary fibre, 4 g sugar), 33 mg chol, 109 mg sodium, 320 mg potassium. % RDI: 1% calcium, 7% iron, 14% vit A, 13% vit C, 26% folate.

Grilled Parmesan Corn

HANDS-ON TIME	TOTAL TIME	MAKES
25 MINUTES	25 MINUTES	6 SERVINGS

Whisk together butter, oil, paprika and salt; set aside.

Place corn cobs on greased grill over medium-high heat; close lid and grill, turning occasionally, for 8 minutes. Brush corn cobs with some of the butter mixture; grill, turning and brushing with remaining butter mixture, until grill-marked and tender, 12 to 15 minutes. Sprinkle with Parmesan and parsley.

1 tbsp	butter, melted
1 tbsp	olive oil
½ tsp	smoked or sweet paprika
pinch	salt
6	corn cobs, husked
½ cup	grated Parmesan cheese
1 tbsp	chopped fresh parsley

NUTRITIONAL INFORMATION, PER SERVING: about 127 cal, 5 g pro, 7 g total fat (3 g sat. fat), 13 g carb (1 g dietary fibre, 2 g sugar), 12 mg chol, 150 mg sodium, 142 mg potassium. % RDI: 9% calcium, 4% iron, 5% vit A, 7% vit C, 11% folate.

Grilled Corn
WITH SRIRACHA AIOLI

HANDS-ON TIME	TOTAL TIME	MAKES
25 MINUTES	25 MINUTES	8 SERVINGS

SRIRACHA AIOLI

3	egg yolks
2 tsp	Dijon mustard
1	clove garlic, finely grated or pressed
¼ tsp	salt
pinch	pepper
½ cup	vegetable oil
¼ cup	extra-virgin olive oil
1 tbsp	chopped fresh cilantro (optional)
2 tsp	sriracha
1 tsp	red wine vinegar

GRILLED CORN

8	corn cobs, husked

SRIRACHA AIOLI In bowl, whisk together egg yolks, mustard, garlic, salt and pepper. Gradually whisk in vegetable oil until mixture is pale yellow and thickened. Gradually whisk in olive oil. Stir in cilantro (if using), sriracha and vinegar. *(Make-ahead: Refrigerate in airtight container for up to 5 days.)*

GRILLED CORN Place corn cobs on lightly greased grill over medium heat; close lid and grill, turning occasionally and brushing each with 1 tbsp of the aioli during last 5 minutes of grilling, until kernels are deep yellow and tender, 15 to 20 minutes. Serve with remaining aioli.

NUTRITIONAL INFORMATION, PER SERVING: about 388 cal, 7 g pro, 25 g total fat (3 g sat. fat), 43 g carb (5 g dietary fibre, 6 g sugar), 72 mg chol, 134 mg sodium, 430 mg potassium. % RDI: 1% calcium, 10% iron, 8% vit A, 18% vit C, 40% folate.

VARIATION
Corn With Sriracha Mayonnaise
If the raw egg yolks in the aioli are a concern for you, omit egg yolks, salt, vegetable oil, olive oil and red wine vinegar; replace with 1 cup prepared mayonnaise.

Charred Corn & Tomato Salad
WITH CHIPOTLE VINAIGRETTE

HANDS-ON TIME	TOTAL TIME	MAKES
30 MINUTES	30 MINUTES	8 SERVINGS

CHIPOTLE VINAIGRETTE Whisk together oil, vinegar, chipotle chili, honey, adobo sauce, salt and pepper; set aside. *(Make-ahead: Refrigerate in airtight container for up to 24 hours.)*

SALAD Brush corn cobs with 2 tsp of the vinaigrette. Place on greased grill over medium heat; close lid and grill, turning occasionally, until charred and tender, 15 to 20 minutes.

Cut kernels from corn cobs. In large bowl, toss together corn kernels, tomatoes, parsley, basil, chives and remaining vinaigrette. Serve warm.

NUTRITIONAL INFORMATION, PER SERVING: about 130 cal, 2 g pro, 8 g total fat (1 g sat. fat), 16 g carb (2 g dietary fibre, 5 g sugar), 0 mg chol, 102 mg sodium, 341 mg potassium. % RDI: 2% calcium, 7% iron, 16% vit A, 33% vit C, 19% folate.

CHIPOTLE VINAIGRETTE

¼ cup	olive oil
3 tbsp	red wine vinegar
1	canned chipotle chili in adobo sauce, minced
2 tsp	liquid honey
1 tsp	adobo sauce
¼ tsp	each salt and pepper

SALAD

2	corn cobs, husked
1.25 kg	tomatoes, seeded and cut in 1½-inch chunks
½ cup	fresh parsley, torn
½ cup	fresh basil, torn
¼ cup	chopped fresh chives

TIP FROM THE TEST KITCHEN
Depending on the variety, some tomatoes can make salads watery. Seeding them first removes much of their liquid.

Grilled Vegetable Pouches

HANDS-ON TIME	TOTAL TIME	MAKES
10 MINUTES	30 MINUTES	6 TO 8 SERVINGS

8	carrots, sliced
8	small new potatoes
4	small onions, chopped
2 tbsp	vegetable oil
2 tbsp	chopped fresh herbs (such as basil, oregano and parsley)
½ **tsp**	each salt and pepper

Place two 18-inch lengths of greased heavy-duty foil (or double thickness of regular foil) on work surface. Divide carrots, potatoes and onions among foil pieces; sprinkle with oil, herbs, salt and pepper. Bring together 2 opposite ends of foil and fold to seal, leaving room inside for expansion; fold in remaining sides to seal.

Place on grill over medium-high heat; close lid and grill, turning once, until tender, about 20 minutes.

NUTRITIONAL INFORMATION, PER EACH OF 8 SERVINGS: about 168 cal, 3 g pro, 4 g total fat (trace sat. fat), 32 g carb (4 g dietary fibre), 0 mg chol, 200 mg sodium. % RDI: 4% calcium, 12% iron, 182% vit A, 25% vit C, 11% folate.

TIP FROM THE TEST KITCHEN
You can cook many other vegetables in foil using this method. Try broccoli, zucchini, green beans, sugar snap peas and sweet peppers.

Grilled Baked Potatoes
WITH GREEN ONION SOUR CREAM

HANDS-ON TIME	TOTAL TIME	MAKES
20 MINUTES	1¼ HOURS	6 SERVINGS

p.44

POTATOES Using fork, prick potatoes all over. Bake in 400°F oven, turning once, until tender, 50 to 60 minutes. Set aside until cool enough to handle. *(Make-ahead: Let cool completely; refrigerate in airtight container for up to 3 days. Continue with recipe, adding 5 minutes to cook time.)*

Halve potatoes lengthwise; brush cut sides with oil and sprinkle with salt. Place, cut sides down, on greased grill over medium heat; leave lid open and grill, turning once, until grill-marked, about 15 minutes.

GREEN ONION SOUR CREAM While potatoes are cooking, in small bowl, stir together sour cream, green onions and pepper. *(Make-ahead: Refrigerate in airtight container for up to 3 days.)* Serve with potatoes.

NUTRITIONAL INFORMATION, PER SERVING: about 208 cal, 5 g pro, 4 g total fat (2 g sat. fat), 39 g carb (4 g dietary fibre, 2 g sugar), 4 mg chol, 27 mg sodium, 982 mg potassium. % RDI: 4% calcium, 14% iron, 2% vit A, 30% vit C, 25% folate.

POTATOES
3	large baking potatoes (such as russet)
1 tbsp	olive oil
pinch	salt

GREEN ONION SOUR CREAM
⅓ cup	sour cream
2	green onions, minced
¼ tsp	pepper

TIP FROM THE TEST KITCHEN
Don't want to heat your oven? Bake the pricked potatoes on the indirect heat of your outdoor grill. Place on 1 rack of 2-burner barbecue or on centre rack of 3-burner barbecue. Heat remaining burner(s) to medium-high heat; close lid and grill, turning potatoes once, until tender, 50 to 60 minutes.

Quinoa Salad
WITH GRILLED SUMMER VEGETABLES

HANDS-ON TIME	TOTAL TIME	MAKES
45 MINUTES	45 MINUTES	4 TO 6 SERVINGS

1 cup	quinoa
3 tbsp	olive oil
2 tbsp	red wine vinegar
1	canned chipotle pepper in adobo sauce, minced
2 tsp	liquid honey
½ tsp	ground cumin
¼ tsp	each salt and pepper
1	each sweet red pepper and sweet yellow pepper, seeded and quartered
1	zucchini, cut lengthwise in ½-inch thick strips
12	asparagus spears, trimmed
½ cup	light feta cheese, crumbled
¼ cup	toasted pumpkin seeds
3 tbsp	chopped fresh cilantro

Soak quinoa in cold water for 3 minutes; drain in fine-mesh sieve. In saucepan, bring 1½ cups salted water to boil; stir in quinoa and return to boil. Reduce heat to low; cover and simmer until no liquid remains, 12 to 15 minutes. Remove from heat and fluff with fork; cover and let stand for 5 minutes. Spread on small tray and let cool for 10 minutes.

Whisk together oil, vinegar, chipotle pepper, honey, cumin, salt and pepper.

In large bowl, add red and yellow peppers, zucchini, asparagus and 3 tbsp of the vinaigrette; toss to coat. Place on greased grill over medium heat; close lid and grill until charred and tender, 4 to 6 minutes for asparagus, 10 to 12 minutes for peppers and zucchini. Cut into large chunks and return to bowl.

Add remaining vinaigrette, the quinoa, half of the feta, the pumpkin seeds and cilantro; toss. Sprinkle with remaining feta. Serve immediately.

NUTRITIONAL INFORMATION, PER EACH OF 6 SERVINGS: about 258 cal, 9 g pro, 13 g total fat (3 g sat. fat), 28 g carb (4 g dietary fibre), 6 mg chol, 343 mg sodium, 476 mg potassium. % RDI: 7% calcium, 31% iron, 18% vit A, 110% vit C, 34% folate.

TIP FROM THE TEST KITCHEN
Although most quinoa in the grocery store has been washed to remove a natural resin that has a bitter flavour, it's a good idea to rinse it again, just in case.

Maple Balsamic
Bok Choy Salad

HANDS-ON TIME	TOTAL TIME	MAKES
20 MINUTES	20 MINUTES	6 SERVINGS

MAPLE BALSAMIC GLAZE In small saucepan, cook onion, maple syrup, vinegar, garlic and rosemary over medium-high heat until syrupy and reduced by half, about 12 minutes. Strain through fine-mesh sieve; discard solids.

BOK CHOY In large bowl, add bok choy, oil and salt; toss to coat. Place on greased grill or grill pan over medium-high heat; close lid and grill, turning occasionally, until grill-marked, about 5 minutes. Transfer to serving plate. Drizzle with maple syrup mixture. Sprinkle with goat cheese and pumpkin seeds.

NUTRITIONAL INFORMATION, PER SERVING: about 141 cal, 6 g pro, 7 g total fat (2 g sat. fat), 15 g carb (2 g dietary fibre, 11 g sugar), 5 mg chol, 197 mg sodium, 744 mg potassium. % RDI: 18% calcium, 22% iron, 78% vit A, 77% vit C, 35% folate.

MAPLE BALSAMIC GLAZE

half	onion, chopped
¼ cup	maple syrup
¼ cup	balsamic vinegar
1	clove garlic, sliced
1	sprig fresh rosemary

BOK CHOY

8	heads Shanghai bok choy, halved
1 tbsp	olive oil
¼ tsp	salt
½ cup	crumbled soft goat cheese
¼ cup	pumpkin seeds, toasted

TIP FROM THE TEST KITCHEN
Try this glaze on roasted squash and other vegetables or on grilled chicken, pork tenderloin or lamb.

Grilled Asparagus & Halloumi Salad

HANDS-ON TIME	TOTAL TIME	MAKES
15 MINUTES	15 MINUTES	4 SERVINGS

1	bunch asparagus (about 450 g), trimmed
1	pkg (250 g) halloumi cheese, cut in ½-inch thick slices
1	head Boston lettuce, torn
4 cups	torn romaine lettuce
¾ cup	cherry tomatoes, halved
2 tbsp	olive oil
2 tsp	red wine vinegar
pinch	each salt and pepper

Place asparagus on greased grill over medium-high heat; close lid and grill, turning often, 2 minutes.

Add halloumi; close lid and grill, turning once, until asparagus is tender and slightly grill-marked and halloumi is grill-marked, 3 to 4 minutes.

Meanwhile, on platter, combine Boston lettuce, romaine lettuce and cherry tomatoes. Whisk together oil, vinegar, salt and pepper; toss with salad. Top with asparagus and halloumi.

NUTRITIONAL INFORMATION, PER SERVING: about 304 cal, 16 g pro, 24 g total fat (11 g sat. fat), 9 g carb (3 g dietary fibre, 3 g sugar), 63 mg chol, 769 mg sodium, 458 mg potassium. % RDI: 36% calcium, 13% iron, 86% vit A, 37% vit C, 98% folate.

TIP FROM THE TEST KITCHEN
Halloumi, a Middle Eastern cheese, is one of the few that holds its shape when grilled.

INDEX

GRILLED STEAK AND ASPARAGUS SALAD
(P.47)

CONTRIBUTORS

RECIPES

All recipes were developed and Tested Till Perfect by the Canadian Living Test Kitchen

PHOTOGRAPHY

JEFF COULSON cover; back cover (left, top; left, second from top; left, bottom; centre; right); p.9, 10, 15, 21, 22, 27, 31, 36, 39, 40, 43, 44, 49, 50, 53, 59, 60, 65, 66, 69, 70, 76, 81, 82, 87, 91, 92, 97, 103, 107, 108, 112, 117, 118, 121, 129, 141, 142, 151 and 158

YVONNE DUIVENVOORDEN p.75, 104, 122 and 136

JOE KIM p.88

EDWARD POND p.28

JODI PUDGE p.54

RYAN SZULC back cover (left, third from top); p.130

JAMES TSE p.149

MAYA VISNYEI p.16, 98, 111 and 135

FOOD STYLING

ASHLEY DENTON cover; p.27, 28, 40, 43, 75, 82, 104, 121, 122, 129 and 136

MICHAEL ELLIOTT/JUDY INC. p.16, 54, 98, 111 and 135

ADELE HAGEN back cover (left, top; right); p.21, 31, 81, 103, 108, 112, 142 and 151

DAVID GRENIER back cover (left, second from top); p.9, 36, 91, 97 and 141

MATTHEW KIMURA p.117 and 118

LUCIE RICHARD p.159

HEATHER SHAW p.70

CLAIRE STUBBS back cover (left, bottom; centre); p.15, 22, 39, 49, 50, 53, 59, 60, 66, 69, 87, 88, 92 and 107

MELANIE STUPARYK p.10, 44 and 158

NICOLE YOUNG back cover (left, third from top); p.65, 76 and 130

PROP STYLING

LAURA BRANSON cover; back cover (left, top; left, second from top; right); p.10, 21, 27, 31, 43, 70, 81, 103, 108, 112, 142, 151 and 159

AURALIE BRYCE p.141

CATHERINE DOHERTY back cover (left, bottom; centre); p.27, 49, 50, 54, 59, 65, 66, 76 and 92

JENNIFER EVANS p.16, 98, 111 and 135

MADELEINE JOHARI back cover (left, third from top); p.10, 22, 39, 44, 53, 60, 69, 87, 88, 107, 130 and 158

SASHA SEYMOUR p.36, 40, 75, 82, 97, 104, 117, 118, 121, 122, 129 and 136

CAROLYN SOUCH/JUDY INC. p.91

About Our Nutrition Information

To meet nutrient needs each day, moderately active women aged 25 to 49 need about 1,900 calories, 51 g protein, 261 g carbohydrate, 25 to 35 g fibre and not more than 63 g total fat (21 g saturated fat). Men and teenagers usually need more. Canadian sodium intake of approximately 3,500 mg daily should be reduced, whereas the intake of potassium from food sources should be increased to 4,700 mg per day. The percentage of recommended daily intake (% RDI) is based on the values used for Canadian food labels for calcium, iron, vitamins A and C, and folate.

Figures are rounded off. They are based on the first ingredient listed when there is a choice and do not include optional ingredients or those with no specified amounts.

ABBREVIATIONS

cal = calories
pro = protein
carb = carbohydrate
sat. fat = saturated fat
chol = cholesterol

**SESAME CHICKEN AND RADISH SKEWERS
WITH ORANGE SALAD**
(P.115)

Canadian Living

Complete your collection of Tested-Till-Perfect recipes!

The Ultimate Cookbook

The Complete Chicken Book
The Complete Chocolate Book
The Complete Preserving Book

400-Calorie Dinners
Dinner in 30 Minutes or Less
Essential Barbecue
Essential Salads
Fish & Seafood
Make It Ahead!
Make It Chocolate!
Pasta & Noodles
Sweet & Simple

New Slow Cooker Favourites

The Special Occasions Cookbook

The Affordable Feasts Collection
The Appetizer Collection
The Barbecue Collection
The International Collection
The One Dish Collection
The Slow Cooker Collection
The Vegetarian Collection

150 Essential Beef, Pork & Lamb Recipes
150 Essential Salads
150 Essential Whole Grain Recipes

Available wherever books are sold or online at
canadianliving.com/books